Black Belt Power

INSPIRATIONAL STORIES BY EXTRAORDINARY MARTIAL ARTISTS

Published by
Master Mel Productions
355 Lexington Press
New York, NY 10017

Manufactured in the United States of America, or in the United Kingdom when distributed elsewhere.

Meyer, Melodee
Black Belt Power—Inspirational Stories by Extraordinary Martial Artists
ISBN:
    Paperback: 978-1-938015-57-1
    eBook: 978-1-938015-58-8

Cover design and photo by: Melodee Meyer/Joe Potter
Interior design: Scribe Inc.
Photo of Melodee Meyer by: Stephanie Westover

A portion of the proceeds of this book will go to support AHA!— transforming the world by empowering teens to create peaceful and connected communities. www.AHAsb.org

Author's URL: MasterMel.com

CONTENTS

FOREWORD

Larry Broughton

> When a man is beaten, tormented, and
> defeated . . . he is ready to learn something.
>
> —*Ralph Waldo Emerson*

If you've been awake during the past decade, you've recognized that societal tensions seem to be nearing a boiling point. More and more clashes seem to be breaking out between the haves and have-nots and between whites and people of color, and sadly, anger seems to be the mood of the decade. When we turn to our elected officials for guidance, they seem flabbergasted and ill-prepared to lead. It's time to start learning something.

I'm of the belief that neither government nor our elected officials have the capability or the courage to lead us to higher ground. There is, however, a vital role to be played by martial artists with influence who believe in the greatness of mankind and the power of human potential. It was nearly thirty-five years ago when I learned that peace, brotherhood, and tranquility were among some of the most powerful tenets of the martial way. It was then that I recognized the dichotomy of martial arts—by learning to destroy, one learns not to destroy. The book you hold in your hands includes some of the powerful answers needed to improve our own lives, as well as the lives of those we serve and love. And because of the powerful ripple effect of these lessons, society will be improved, enlightened, and restored.

In any endeavor, discipline, practice, or pursuit for high-achievement, best practices emerge from the "great ones" in that field. Since the history of martial arts goes back millennia, it's natural that there would be countless *great ones* who have made a lasting impact on its study, on civilization, and on the society it serves. When we connect the dots of the *great ones*, we recognize that the greatest marital artists share five common traits: they train often, they're lifelong learners, they're focused, they practice without ego, and they inspire others toward greater versions of themselves.

I was first introduced to Master Melodee Meyer several years ago at a business marketing seminar where I was presenting. What struck me most was the vitality and *joie de vivre* she exuded. Since that time, I've had the honor of getting to know her on a personal and professional level: I've had dinner at her home with her family; I've spoken to instructors and students at her dojo; and I've discussed her impact on her community with other business leaders. Her desire to make a positive global contribution by inspiring others toward a more awakened, vibrant, and enlightened state will have a multigenerational impact for good. Based on the criteria listed above, Master Mel is, indeed, one of the *great ones*. Her creation, *Black Belt Power: Inspirational Stories by Extraordinary Martial Artists*, inspires readers to grow beyond their current position and awareness to imagine how life could be; it provides a road map on how life shall be if these principles are actively applied.

Some of the contributions found herein are from living legends and celebrity martial artists, while others are from less prominent though equally important Black Belts who selflessly serve to instill honor and integrity in their charges. All the stories, however, are powerful, from practitioners who study traditional forms of martial arts to innovators who have improvised and adapted multiple styles. They all have a story, and it's all in here: honesty and vulnerability, fear and fearlessness, courage and playfulness, and tragedy and triumph. There are lessons for modern life to be learned from every story told.

I recall an interview with Grand Master Jhoon Rhee more than thirty years ago in which he stated there are three types of people in the world: those who watch things happen, those who make things happen, and those who don't even know what's happening. He went on to ask, "Which type are you?" That simple question has tumbled around in my brain all these years, and it has inspired me to take action toward a life of adventure, leadership, and high achievement. I'm indebted to Grand Master Rhee for that simple—yet powerful—awakening.

I'm certain you'll find nuggets of truth in each of the stories in this book that will inspire and awaken your imagination. I encourage you to take a few minutes to reflect on each one . . . and then, if the nugget resonates with your spirit, set intentions on implementing that lesson into your routine and life—and prepare to be amazed.

A word of caution, though: if you apply and embrace the lessons from this powerful book, you will *not* be magically transported to a higher plane of consciousness. You *will*, however, become a greater, new-and-improved version of yourself, filled with light, freedom, clarity, and purpose to serve and thrive. Though the journey will, at times, seem rugged and long, don't despair; just when the caterpillar thought the world was over, it became a butterfly.

Larry Broughton is an award-winning entrepreneur and CEO, best-selling author, Black Belt, former US Army Green Beret, and nationally acclaimed keynote speaker. He is the founder of yoogozi. com, broughtonHOTELS, and BROUGHTONadvisory. He makes regular appearances on radio and television networks to discuss personal development, entrepreneurship, strengths-based team building, and the leadership gap he sees growing across America.
www.LarryBroughton.me

Introduction

Melodee Meyer

A black belt is just a band of cloth.

And yet what a black belt represents is so powerful, so iconic, that everyone recognizes its significance immediately.

Even as a child, before I knew anything about Karate, I knew the black belt was something special. I assumed it gave the bearer some kind of superpower. To me, a black belt was something magical that could not be explained because it was (ahem) . . . an "ancient Chinese secret."

In martial arts, where belts are used to rank its practitioners, the black belt is an achievement that denotes a great deal of skill and a certain level of expertise, dependent on the style and requirements of that specific art.

I love the traditional story of the black belt's origin. Before buttons or zippers were invented, ties and belts were used to keep clothes in place. So, in Asia where martial artists trained in white kimonos, their belts became dirty, remained unwashed, and darkened with time. According to the story, it was clear who the senior students were by how dark their belts were.

Now, whether this unhygienic tale is true or not, I like the mental image of a belt used for so many years that it eventually turns black. I like the idea that rank was based on the amount of time and effort one invested. I like that the color represented the natural progression of consistency over time.

Today the black belt is awarded ceremoniously as a high achievement worthy of great celebration, as it should. To earn a black belt takes years of study, practice, and training—all of which stem from the inception of an incredible commitment to a worthy challenge.

Earning a black belt is one thing. *Being* a Black Belt is quite another. Anyone who passed a black belt test and then quit training never became a Black Belt. Black Belts don't quit. In some traditions, the true martial arts journey *begins* at black belt.

When one earns a black belt, it means one has completed a certain curriculum; essentially, one has learned the basics. One continues training in the basics in order to master them, and therein lies the art. Black Belts use their training to create a better version of themselves.

This book might not make you want to earn a black belt (although I hope it does!) or think more highly of those who have (although I know you will!); it's real purpose is to inspire you to become the best version of yourself. Through these stories, I hope you are motivated to break through the obstacles in your path, step past your limitations and your limiting beliefs, and get a taste of your inner strength, your own power.

Power is not force. It is not the exertion of control over others. True power is the space in which we can choose our next action or reaction. True power is the energy of being confident of our choices and our abilities. I believe it is meant to be our natural state.

As we grow up, there is a tendency to give up our power and become victims of our circumstances. Many of us remain trapped there until the day we choose a different outcome—until we choose to step into our power.

The authors in this book are all ordinary people who, like you, know a little something about struggles and challenges. In these Black Belts' stories, they will reveal the steps they took to experience their own power.

Some of these stories will make you laugh; some will make you cry. Some of the stories may even have you sitting on the edge of your seat, but more importantly, one of these stories could crack open your heart and allow you to release outdated beliefs about what is possible.

It's time. And you are worth it.

I was extremely humbled and honored to collect these stories from some of the most amazing people I have ever met. May you recognize yourself in these pages as you learn a few "ancient Chinese secrets" of your own.

The Black Belt Way

Steve Selby

On a return flight from the Virgin Islands in the summer of 2007, I encountered fear like never before. Our departure was already delayed by about fifteen minutes when two thirty-something Middle Eastern men entered the plane and proceeded toward the back of the plane.

The plane began to taxi, and the two men appeared very nervous and paranoid. They attempted to sit in random seats until the flight attendant guided them to their assigned seats. One of the men sat in the middle seat between my girlfriend and I. The other man sat in front of him.

Both men were sweating profusely and constantly fidgeting in their seats. They were conversing loudly in what sounded like Arabic. The terrified faces of the other passengers confirmed that we were not alone with our fears.

The man sitting next to me kept removing his glasses to wipe the pouring sweat from his face and neck and then take off his watch and wipe his wrists and arms. He kept opening and closing his fists on the arm rests as he rocked aggressively back and forth in his seat, all the while looking straight ahead and loud talking.

Both men would grab their in-flight magazines, flip through the pages nervously, and replace them. They kept repeating the same nervous routine over and over as their voices escalated to the point of yelling. The other passengers were freaking out and women were crying.

I asked the man to my left if he would switch places with my girlfriend. He just stared straight ahead and said, "No!" in an angry, forceful tone. My girlfriend was scared and her eyes were welling up.

It was time to take action.

> KRAMER: "Kara-te, Jerry. Kara-te. The lifetime pursuit of balance and harmony."
>
> JERRY: "But with punching and kicking."
>
> (*Seinfeld,* Season 8, Episode 135)

I was born and raised in Dallas, Texas. My dad was a lieutenant commander during World War II and a collegiate boxing champion. He began teaching me to box when I was three years old. I took my first Karate class at age ten. In seventh grade I had to fight two kids at a time every day to keep my lunch money. I hated bullies!

I heard about the Texas Karate Institute and Karate champion Allen Steen. I heard that if you learned Karate there, you could beat anyone. I envisioned myself learning to fight like Billy Jack. I begged my parents to sign me up and promised I wouldn't quit. I went six days a week.

I made orange belt in three weeks, competed as a green belt in three months, and was a Brown Belt within the year. After competing for three years as a Brown Belt, I was allowed to test for black belt. I was the only one of the three candidates that day who the twenty or so members of the black belt board passed unanimously.

I could finally fight as a Black Belt!

> Martial arts is about conditioning your mind, body, and spirit to be prepared, and able to take action.

> —*S. Selby*

So here I was, on a plane full of nervous, frightened passengers and a crying girlfriend, taxiing towards the runway with two crazed men acting like lit fuses. I thought, "Time's up!"

I immediately walked up to the front of plane. The flight attendants looked terrified, and one was crying. I said to them, "Tell the captain we have two terrorists on the plane and we need to get back to the gate immediately!"

"We've been watching them and are very concerned," one of the flight attendants answered. "The Captain already knows." I returned to my seat.

The two men were becoming more and more intense. I looked at the man next to me and thought, "THIS IS IT! If we take off, we're done."

So I began banging my knee hard against his leg, over and over, at least a dozen times, staring him right in the face the whole time. I knew that I needed to get him to make a move while we were still on the ground.

He never once looked at me. He just stared straight ahead and kept talking loudly to his friend. My girlfriend was clearly terrified, and I mouthed silently to her, "Do you want off this plane?" She quickly nodded yes.

I went back up to the front of the plane, where all three flight attendants were now crying. I said to the lead attendant, "Tell the captain that we want off this plane now! Tell him that I've made a direct threat to take out either of these men if they attempt to leave their seats." She went right into the cockpit.

A few seconds later she came out and said, "We don't want to cause alarm, so we will announce that we have passengers on the wrong plane and must return to the gate."

The plane returned to the gate and as we were escorted up the ramp I noticed more passengers exiting the plane. Two visibly shaken young men approached me and extended their hands. "Thank you, sir, for what you did. We were scared to death watching the two men in the front of the plane."

In the *front* of the plane? I learned that there were two more men at the front of the plane behaving the exact same way.

Later we learned that the crew refused to fly with those men on board, and the flight was eventually cancelled.

The following Monday morning my girlfriend and I got a visit from the FBI and Homeland Security. They questioned us about the incident and thanked us for taking action. They said they couldn't give us any details, but the four men had been removed from the plane and wouldn't be flying again anytime soon. They also said that they had been monitoring similar activity that day on the West Coast as well.

Martial arts saved our lives that day—by recognizing the threat, and acting preemptively, no physical force was necessary. The highest level of martial arts is mental, where you don't have to engage physically. Confidence comes from competence, and martial arts training plus real life experiences produced the confidence and courage to take the lead and action I believe it was courage and leadership skills developed through martial arts training that turned the plane around that day and brought us to safety.

Training in martial arts is more than learning techniques. It's about developing the mind, body and spirit through rigorous training. It's having courage and quick thinking, even in the face of fear. It's standing up for what's right, even if it's unpopular. And it's doing what you need to do, when you need to do it—that's the black belt way.

Steve Selby has been teaching martial arts since 1976. He trained under the Allen Steen Texas "Blood and Guts" Karate System and competed extensively through the seventies and early eighties. He's the founder of Dallas Martial Arts and serves as vice chairman of the American Karate Black Belt Association.

www.SteveSelby.com

Indomitable Spirit with Courage on the Side!

Diane Reeve

Indomitable spirit is my favorite character trait. It's the ability to keep going despite extraordinarily difficult circumstances. Actually, it's more like getting through the situation and coming out ahead. For that you also need a generous helping of courage on the side.

I started training in 1985 using a system with a rich history of forefathers. One was Allen Steen, "The Father of Texas Blood and Guts Karate." Texas Karate was so tough that Bill "Superfoot" Wallace once said, "A point in Texas Karate is like capital murder in California." Steen was the only guy to ever defeat Chuck Norris and Joe Lewis in the same tournament.

Here is a story about what indomitable spirit is *not*.

In the final moments of a black belt exam, a candidate had been through a demanding physical and psychological battle. He had lasted for hours, demonstrating techniques with power and accuracy. Sparring was the last and most difficult part. Already exhausted and battered, he fought single rounds, then fought four or five at a time. As he stood praying that the exam was over, Steen queried, "Are you ready for one more match?" Falling to his knees on the floor, he cried, "No, no, I can't. I can't do anymore!"

Steen silently raised the exam sheet. Slowly his paper was ripped in half. The test was over—the man had failed.

He didn't fail because of incorrect or weak techniques. He failed because he didn't have what it took to be a black belt: indomitable spirit.

On my black belt test, I sure knew what *not* to do! I knew not to quit. And that was just the beginning for me. As I continued training, I was knocked down, bruised and had some bones broken. That's just part of training. What mattered was to *never, ever quit*!

In 2006 I was a fifth-degree Black Belt and owned a martial art school. I'd taught plenty of people about indomitable spirit. And I was about to face the biggest test of it in my own life.

A handsome Frenchman had swept me off my feet. We had been together for over four years and were building a house together; we planned to live happily ever. Unfortunately, I learned of his infidelity and let him go. I was devastated.

Even worse, I had to have surgery to remove precancerous cells due to the HPV he had given me! For the next six months, I had multiple health problems: fatigue, irregular blood work, an unclear diagnosis. I wondered how long it would be before someone told me, "You have cancer."

When the economy took a downturn, my school did, too. Next came more devastating blows. The good news was that I didn't have cancer. The bad news was that I had AIDS. I was sure I was going to die. I had no immune system, and I taught dozens of little germ factories every day. Insurance wouldn't cover the medicines I needed to survive. I was barely making ends meet. Then I learned that my Frenchman not only gave me HIV, he knew he had it, and he lied! My prince charming was the prince of evil.

When I got my diagnosis, I fell to my knees! When insurance didn't cover what I needed, I curled up in a ball and cried. When I found out my former boyfriend lied, knew all along, and didn't care enough to protect me, did I give up? NO! Not only no—hell, no! I got mad. I picked myself up and took action.

I learned there were other women who had been involved with the Frenchman, and I teamed up with one of them. We knew what he did was wrong, and we knew there was no doubt he was continuing his incredibly selfish rampage. We couldn't let him continue to hurt women, so we went to the police. I thought that would stop him.

Although the detective was very sympathetic, he informed us that it would take not two but maybe as many as *five* victims to come forward in order to get charged filed. And that's when I really needed courage. I knew I had a choice. I could go back to my house, close the school, and give up. Or I could have the courage to do something. Courage and indomitable spirit go hand in hand. Courage is doing what's right even though you're afraid.

It had taken courage to walk into the police station, but it took more to go and talk to all this man's potential victims—if anyone had told him, my life would have been in danger. I also knew that reliving it all in court would be traumatic, but I did it anyway, because that's what Black Belt do!

Eventually ten of us came forward. There were at least fifty more.

The case made national headlines. I made appearances on *20/20* and *Oprah*. But there was a final crossroad. Both shows offered to let us use pseudonyms and disguises because of the stigma surrounding HIV. Most of the women did.

If I disclosed the fact that I had HIV on national TV, I would be risking my business. I might be forced to close the doors. However, I learned that there hadn't been any documentation of a sports transmission case of HIV. I certainly didn't do anything wrong. I could educate millions of people about the disease and warn millions of women about the dangers of trusting the wrong person, plus fight against stigma of a misunderstood disease.

I was terrified! But I went on television with no disguise and used my real name. Out of 230 students, only one left. *One!* After the television appearances, a dad came up to me in his fatigues and stuck out his hand. "Last week I got back from Afghanistan. I just had to tell you that you are the bravest person I know." Wow! I had it! Indomitable spirit with a side of courage!

If I hadn't been a Black Belt, I would not be here right now. All along I kept thinking, *Nobody was going to tear my paper in half!*

Diane Reeve, the author of Standing Strong, *has been called "the new face of HIV." Her story has been the subject of episodes of 20/20, Oprah, and others. She owns Vision Martial Arts Center in Plano, Texas. HIV advocacy and education has become her mission as she delivers inspiring messages nationwide.*

www.DateStronger.com

Josh Arcemont

Being a martial arts instructor, the one question I get asked the most is: "How did you get started in martial arts?" The answer is simple—I walked into a martial arts school and signed up. The real question is *why* I got started and why I stayed with it.

In elementary school I was a shy, introverted boy with a speech impediment. I had a tough time pronouncing my "Rs" correctly. While other kids my age went to art class, I had to go to speech therapy. I had always wanted to try out for our school plays, but I was embarrassed by my speech impediment.

I was the shortest kid in my third grade class, and because of that my nickname on the playground was "Shrimp." I wasn't particularly good at sports so I never got picked to be on any of the teams. My confidence was very low. I tried my hand at different sports—soccer, baseball, swimming, tennis, and even bowling! I didn't excel at any of them.

I tried going the artistic route, playing the viola and the drums in middle school, but none of these activities really sparked my interest, and I ended up quitting them all. By the time I was in high school, I didn't play any team sports, I wasn't involved with any school organizations, and I felt like just another kid lost in the shuffle.

The summer before my sophomore year, my family moved to a new city. I looked at this as an opportunity to reinvent myself and start with a clean slate. The kids in this new school didn't know me as the "shrimp" with the speech impediment who wasn't on any sports teams. I decided I could be anyone I wanted to be!

I had always had a fascination with martial arts, so I decided to give it a try. At the time, I thought it was because I wanted to learn how to fight. What I didn't realize was that I was starving for self-confidence and self-esteem.

I began training and fumbled along in the beginning like all white belts do. Almost immediately I began to make new friends, and they helped me with my kicks and with learning my forms.

Not long after I began, I tested for my first belt and was awarded "Best Tester" by my instructor. He handed me a trophy in front of my peers and praised my efforts. Immediately my self-worth and self-esteem started to grow. Finally people were taking notice of me, and my effort was being recognized.

This spilled over into my social life. I became more outgoing, which earned me new friends. I tried out for the school play and won a part as the fight choreographer in our school's version of *West Side Story*. I also signed up for the school talent show, where I displayed my new martial art skills.

My popularity grew at school, and my new nickname became "The Karate Kid."

By my senior year I had won the Texas State Taekwondo Championship in sparring and forms and was very close to earning my black belt. My life had done a complete 180-degree turn. Kids from my former school couldn't even recognize me anymore. I was confident.

My self-discipline had also improved tremendously. I started to understand the value of hard work and dedication. While other peers of mine where out partying, I was training and winning championships. My entire perception of myself changed over the course of a few short years.

I became an advocate for the martial arts. I wanted to tell everyone what it had done for me. Shortly after earning my black belt, I made the commitment to dedicate my life to teaching martial arts. Martial arts had transformed me, and I couldn't keep it a secret. If it could help me, it could help others, too.

I spent my 20s teaching martial arts and mentoring kids. The satisfaction I got from helping others gave me a purpose in life: helping other people reach their potential and build their self-esteem and confidence. Slowly it became less about me and more about my students. I started working with elementary schools in my community, teaching kids the value of hard work, dedication, and self-discipline. I volunteered my time to be PE teacher for the day. I taught martial arts to kids who would never have had the opportunity otherwise. I began to make an impact—not only on myself, but on my community as well.

Over the next six years I continued to teach martial arts, influencing thousands of students and producing hundreds of black belts. Recently, at a banquet for our students, a man came up to me and shook my hand. As I introduced myself, he looked at me as if to say, "You don't recognize me." He had a beard and so it took a second, but then it hit me. His name was Garret. He was the first student I personally trained all the way to black belt. He was five years old when I first met him, and he was now twenty-three. I hadn't seen him in over twelve years! While shaking my hand, he said, "I need to say thank you, sir! A piece of everything you taught me is still with me today. When life gets hard, and I don't think I can make it, I remember the inspiring things you told me, and the life lessons I learned on the mat. Thank you!"

Martial arts have given me everything—my family, my business, my friendships, and my purpose in life. "Why did I get started, and why did I stay with it?" I started martial arts to improve my life, I stayed because I want to improve the lives of others.

Master Josh Arcemont is an inspirational speaker and founder of HERO Martial Arts Academy. A fifth dan Black Belt, Master Arcemont uses martial arts as a platform to inspire and transform people's lives for the better. www.HeroMAA.com

From Bottom to Top

Dave Wheaton

My report cards said, "David seems smart but . . ." Dot, dot, dot meant a variety of things: "doesn't pay attention," "will not concentrate," "can't sit still"—and my personal favorite, "he's always daydreaming."

This was my story all through grade school and high school. It wasn't that I wouldn't concentrate, I couldn't. My brain was always spinning in a whirlwind of thoughts.

Apparently my gift (and it *is* a gift) is that I am left-handed, mildly dyslexic, and have ADD. I think about things a little differently, have to concentrate on concentrating, and can't sit still for long. If I had been a kid today, I would definitely have been on medication, but I lucked out.

Thank goodness I developed some pretty good negotiating skills and convinced my teachers to pass me each year. In my senior year, I talked two teachers into granting me a passing grade so I could get out of high school. I got out, but barely. I graduated at the very bottom of my class.

The first time I saw Bruce Lee on television jump up and kick out a lightbulb, I was in awe. I had never seen a human being do anything like that before. Of course, today martial arts is an integral part of any action movie, but back then Karate had not hit mainstream America yet. I was amazed at the possibility that anyone could actually move like that.

One day in high school, an upperclassman tripped me and laughed as he rubbed my face in a pile of snow. I was too afraid to say or do anything about it, but I remember wishing that I knew martial arts so I could deal with that bully.

About that time, my best friend John started disappearing every Tuesday and Thursday night and would not tell me what he was up to. After several months he walked into my house and said, "Dave, come out in the driveway; I have to show you something." He asked me to throw a punch at him, and when I did he jumped up in the air, threw a kick, and missed my nose by an inch. He had just gotten his green belt in Tang Soo Do.

John became my first teacher, showing me the basics of how to block, kick, and punch and how to use this to defend myself. I was hooked. I trained with his instructor for a while, then took some lessons in Judo, Aikido, and Muay Thai. What they all had in common was the ability to focus and breathe in order to learn the techniques well.

I had developed a new passion: a passion to learn.

The winter before I graduated high school was a cold one. The ponds in Connecticut were frozen over, and it was an excellent year for skating. I was walking down to our local pond when a car drove by. One of the guys rolled down his window and yelled, "Wheaton, I'm going to kick your ass." The car came to a screeching halt, and the guy jumped out and came running down the road toward me. Normally I would have jumped over the rail and tried to outrun him, but not this time. I wasn't afraid. I stood there, dropped my foot back, and put my hands up, palms forward, just like I had learned in class. I concentrated on my breathing, and for the first time in my life I was totally focused; my mind wasn't jumping around, and I was perfectly calm.

As he closed the distance between us, I kicked him in the belly with a hard front kick. He fell to the ground, whimpering, and I just stood there, ready. After several moments he got up, mumbled a few more threats, and stumbled to the car, which sped away. I continued on my way to the pond, and although

I was shaking a little, shocked, and even a little nervous, I was not scared. Something had shifted deep inside of me.

After high school I continued training in martial arts and eventually met my mentor, Grand Master Tae Hee Yi. Master Yi's classes emphasized the development of strong kicks and punches, low, powerful stances, and unbeatable willpower. He had been in the Korean Special Forces Tiger Division. He trained us like we were in the army—his army—and the Tiger Division patch on the right side of his uniform was a constant reminder of who our teacher was.

Classes were very disciplined and what some may have viewed as severe. Master Yi ran his businesses the same way. He not only taught me the art of Taekwondo, he also taught me how to teach, how to run a martial arts school, and how to build a school from scratch. Working with him really developed my razor-sharp focus. My steel was forged in his fire.

While teaching for him, I decided that I would go back to school and get a degree. Two years later I graduated and was valedictorian of my class. I had gone from the bottom of the class to the top—from a scared kid getting his nose rubbed in the snow to a confident man running a martial arts academy.

The only thing that I had done differently was to start training in the martial arts. The only thing that had changed in me was everything.

Grandmaster Dave Wheaton is the founder of Hapkido International and creator of Dynamic Circle Hapkido. He holds a ninth dan black belt in Hapkido, a seventh dan black belt in Taekwondo, and has been running martial arts schools for over forty years. Dave also holds a Gold Seal Flight Instructor Certificate.
www.MasterWheaton.com

When Life Pushes, Pay Attention

Bill Clark

When I first started my martial arts training, we were taught five tenets: courtesy, integrity, perseverance, self-control, and indomitable spirit. Throughout my life I have used these five tenets to make it through some difficult times. In fact, looking back, my training helped me make it through one of the biggest challenges I've ever had to deal with.

It was a day just like any other, except that day would change my life forever. Life was good; I was a martial arts instructor in my early twenties and I also worked in the printing industry. That day my job required that I climb a ladder twenty-two feet in the air onto the platform of a printing machine.

I don't remember being afraid, but I could have easily died there. Suddenly my hand was pulled into the rollers of the printing machine I was working on. The glove I wore had become tacky enough that it stuck to the moving rollers. I knew I had to turn the machine off. As I reached for the cut-off button, my hair was pulled in the machine, too. Luckily someone on another machine saw my plight and was able to stop it.

Now I was stuck. I couldn't pull my hand out—there was too much pressure. I was over twenty feet in the air, and the only way to reach me was via the ladder. I don't remember much at that point; everything just stopped. There were people everywhere trying to figure out how to remove my hand. It took forty minutes for them to find the right way to remove it from the printer. I wasn't really in pain . . . just shock.

My hand was mangled. It looked like a catcher's mitt, but you could see right through it. All the machines stopped and everyone gathered around me. As I stood there on the platform, stunned, I heard someone yell, "Bill, you're going to have to jump!"

He was right—the only other way down was the ladder, and that took both hands. Now, I was young enough to jump, so I did. I landed okay, but my hand crashed into his hands as they were waiting to catch me, and at that moment the pain started. It was so intense that I didn't speak for maybe four or five hours.

My hand looked so bad that I thought I might as well just die. I was a black belt and an instructor, but I felt like I had no future. People talked to me, and I just didn't want to talk. I thought, *This is my right hand. Everything is over. How can I live without my right hand? There is no coming back from this—what am I going to do now?*

When I finally began to speak, I was not pleasant. I was rude to the doctors, nurses, and even my wife. All I could think about was all the things I would no longer be able to do after this. I wouldn't be able to write. How was I going to teach? Or even drive my car—I wouldn't be able to shift without my right hand. I observed people around me in the hospital who were missing the tips of their fingers; everyone had missing pieces. It was like a war movie. It was horrible.

At that point, I made some decisions. First, I decided that I would not continue to live a life I was dissatisfied with. Most people would have said that I had it good. I had four weeks paid vacation per year because of the union, but I was not satisfied with the life I was living.

As I evaluated my current situation, I realized that I had forgotten my training. I was being unpleasant to everyone trying to help me. I needed to change this *now*. I changed my attitude right then and there. I began being courteous to everyone—after all, they were there to make my situation better. I went from people not wanting to enter my room to continuously having a group of people around me.

My change in attitude changed everything that day. At first the doctors discussed removing parts of my hand and sending me to rehab to regain the use of what was left. They discussed removing at least three of my fingers and part of my wrist. Who could blame them? I wasn't helping the situation being as mean and rude as I was. But when my attitude changed, so did theirs. My level of courtesy changed, and theirs did, too.

There was apparently only one hand surgeon who could fix the damage to my hand, and he was in New York. Within the next twenty-four hours, Dr. Carter was flown to Omaha to attempt to piece my hand back together. He was able to reconstruct it. Now, it's not the prettiest, but you would never be able to tell that I nearly lost it.

After going through rehab, I began teaching again. I could drive my car. I even started playing tennis and golf. All of this happened because I changed my level of courtesy.

Because of martial arts and the tenets we teach, I have been able not only to accomplish all I have, but also keep my right hand. As martial arts instructors, we don't just kick and punch. We teach people to communicate and to become better versions of themselves. It takes both words and actions. We have to self-evaluate and be sure we are going in the direction we desire.

Today's the day that makes all the difference . . . if you do.

Chief Master William Clark is a ninth degree Black Belt and the CEO of Warrior X Fit, Karate America, and Warrior Krav Maga, all headquartered in Jacksonville, Florida. He has twenty-five schools, more than two thousand actively training Black Belts, and is the chairman of the Masters Council of the American Taekwondo Association (ATA).
   www.WarriorBroadcast.com

Healing Heartbreak on the Mat

Sarah White

My heart stopped beating on November 15, 2013—and yet I continued to breathe.

It was the first cold day we experienced during the entire week we were in Mexico. The Baja 1000 was almost over, with less than 200 miles left to go in the race. I rushed as fast as I could to get to a finish line that my fiancé would never reach. You see, he died that day.

My fiancé, Kurt, was a professional off-road endurance racer, and although I knew it was a dangerous sport, he was the best, having won the world championship title several times.

Now the life we had planned and dreamed together was over. The wedding dress hanging in my closet would never be worn. I returned from our vacation without anything that mattered to me. With every minute that passed, I fell deeper and deeper into the worst nightmare possible. I slipped further and further away from the lighthearted, funny, optimistic girl I once had been.

Kurt and I had been a part of each other's lives for ten years, and life without him wasn't comprehensible. I walked around in the body of a person I did not know. Every cell, every atom in me had changed.

I truly felt what it was to be sad. Such a small three letter word now had so much more meaning than I ever knew possible. I couldn't answer a simple question like, "Hi, how are you?" I was a shell. I was stuck and I didn't even want that to change. Any joy made me feel guilty; any light that tried to come into my life made me immediately shut down.

One day Grand Master Wheaton showed up at my door, and at that moment I knew he had come into my life for a reason. As I cried with him about the accident and how I wanted to quit everything in my life, he just listened. I explained that training was just not for me anymore, and he smiled. At that moment I knew I needed to get back on the mat.

Martial arts had been a big part of my life since I was eleven years old. I was very small and shy, and when I started in a new school, I came home crying one day and told my dad about a girl who was picking on me. She had kicked the door in on me in the bathroom. My father had started taking martial arts classes at a local dojo six months earlier, and he decided to take me with him the following week. I was so embarrassed! My friends were taking dance lessons next door, and I didn't want them to know I was taking Karate, so I would run straight in and straight out so no one would see me.

However, it didn't take long before I fell in love with martial arts. After a few months I had so much more confidence, it was crazy. My father and my sensei decided to put me into tournaments, where I loved forms and foot sweeping. I competed in a couple of local events and won first place trophies in both categories! I was so happy and so proud of myself that I wanted to do more!

Those were some of my absolute favorite days with my father. I loved training with him on the mat, and I loved how proud he was of me. I always wanted to do my best and try my hardest to earn his respect.

No matter what was going on, I always had my martial arts. I started teaching Tang Soo Do and then went on to Krav Maga and eventually Hapkido. I enjoyed learning the different arts. It was fun for me to put things together, taking something from this and mixing it with that. I am so glad that girl kicked in the bathroom door that day!

So back to the mat I went.

Not too long after I was back, a man congratulated me on my engagement. At that moment I wanted to run back into my hole screaming, but I fought back the tears, took a deep breath, and just smiled. I knew I had to be strong; I knew I needed to pull it together and grow from this. That was the moment when I knew I could choose one of two paths, and I decided I wasn't going to hide away from life ever again.

I don't know what path I would have taken if I had never come across this passion of mine. I don't expect life to be easy, but thanks to martial arts, I have learned confidence, creativity, perseverance, drive, motivation, and humility, and these empower me to make it through whatever comes. I continue to add things to that list, such as strength, compassion, and inspiration. No matter what happened to me when Kurt died, these key traits are instilled in me, and I find comfort knowing those won't change.

Sarah White is a third-degree Black Belt in American Tang Soo Do and a third-degree Black Belt in Hapkido. She is a kickboxing instructor, a dental hygienist, and the president of The Kurt Caselli Foundation. She hopes her story can inspire others and show them how amazing martial arts truly is.

www.kurtcaselli.com

Fearless: Walking in Purpose

Jeff Quirk

"The only thing we have to fear is fear itself."

—*Franklin D. Roosevelt*

In 2012 I had a great home life, a rewarding personal life, and a successful career. I had no great tragedies from my past that haunted me; I had grown up in a solid, middle-class family where my parents loved me and provided a comfortable, "normal" life for me. I had worked hard to build a high-caliber academy that was filled with smiling, upbeat students and families. Classes were rocking, our billing was solid, and the accolades from loyal customers continued to pour in.

And yet . . . somehow I knew that another level of personal, financial, and professional fulfillment and success were *possible and achievable* for me and for my team. What would I have to unlock in order to truly realize the full power of myself and the company I'd built?

Training in the martial arts conditioned me to actively seek out education and development, so I decided to invest in some exceptional leadership development training for myself and my team. This decision started a new era that has led to unprecedented financial and personal success.

At the very core of our success was that elusive Holy Grail I'd been wondering about and searching for. Hidden in plain sight, shrouded in layers of comfortable success and achievement, I finally realized that I had been making decisions and choices—not always, but enough to make a difference—out of fear.

We learned to start choosing, working, and being on purpose, guided by our values, using powerful communication tools. We uncovered and codified—specifically and explicitly—our Purpose: *"We Inspire People to Believe in Themselves and . . ."* We did the same for our nine core Operating Values.

During this time, I trusted. I believed. *I let go of fear.* In our new era, much of the potency and power of our culture and our work became rooted in our steadfast choice to *not* operate or act out of fear.

It's really that simple—and it's really that difficult.

Fear—in all its forms, from the mild and mundane to the massive and terrifying—is a powerful, master manipulator. Fear lies. Fear knows all the buttons to press. Fear is the warm, safe blanket of complacency and status quo that in reality slowly, quietly suffocates our dreams and our true selves. Sometimes epic stories of transformation and success do not involve a tragic, scarred hero who overcomes seemingly insurmountable odds and obstacles. Sometimes, for people like me, who don't really have it so bad and who are actually doing pretty well, the tragedy is that they might go through their lives believing that this is all there is. For me, fear was the difference between a great life and an unbelievable life; between a successful martial arts academy and an academy whose culture, impact, and financial growth are unlimited.

One of the most profound and impactful eras in my life as a martial artist has been choosing love and hope, choosing to trust and believe in myself and my team at every turn. This is easier said than done.

Recognizing that these old strategies no longer cultivate the vibrant, exciting, "next level of awesome!" life that we want is difficult. As a martial artist, my default outlook on anything challenging or daunting is: "Bring it on!"

I believe this is a key distinction between people who have trained in the martial arts and those who have not.

So what nugget of martial arts wisdom could I humbly offer my students, my staff, and the families that come to my academies that would change their lives far beyond physical training and far beyond titles, belts, and accolades?

"What do you really want to say? Say that."

"What do you really want to do? Do that."

If the answer is "I don't know": "Okay. Well, what is one thing you *do* know?"

Start there—start from even one simple, small truth. Then—and this is *huge*—take *action* based on your purpose, guided by your values. Don't get bogged down in "What ifs" and "Yeah, buts." These are the voices of fear, and they are experts at paralyzing us into inertia. They may have kept us safe and warm and alive in the past, but we simply do not need them anymore. Tell them to take a hike. Resolutely march right into that dark cave and *believe that you will figure it out.*

Get really, really explicit about your Purpose and your Values. Write them down. Carry them around with you. Talk about them to anyone who will listen. Keep doing this even when it feels weird and awkward. Keep doing this even when people look at you with blank stares or laugh at you or respond with dismissive words. Find a great mentor and be open to him or her pushing you way farther than you think you could ever be pushed—this part may not be fun, but do *not* tap out.

Most important of all: Seek out and visit martial arts academies in your area. Meet the staff, talk to the instructors, take some trial classes. Enroll your child at a martial arts academy whose Purpose and Values match your own; this decision alone will impact generations of your family for the better.

I cannot emphasize enough that martial arts training and character development were the foundations that allowed me to seek out and benefit from all the empowering, life-changing aspects of my journey away from fear and toward my true, powerful self. Without martial arts in my life, I would be just another reasonably happy, successful guy. Because of martial arts, I developed the courage to remain an empty vessel—to actively seek out ways I can be better today than I was yesterday.

And finally, trust and believe that you are enough, even when that doesn't seem possible. Choose out of love, not fear. BE On Purpose—be fearless. For me and my team, and anyone who chooses to join us, there is now simply no other way to BE.

Mr. Jeff Quirk is a fifth-degree Black Belt and has competed and won championships at the local, state, and national level. He currently owns two martial arts academies in the metro Milwaukee area and is proud and honored to be a Purpose- and Values-driven leader in the martial arts industry.

www.MyKarateAmerica.com

Martial Arts Are My Life

Brannon Beliso

Over a lifetime of training that began at the age of five, martial arts have been many things to me. At times they have saved my life, at others they have been my life, and today they give me life.

I was a sickly child who stuttered. Kids would tease me because of my speech impediment and say I talked like Porky Pig, an animated character from a Warner Brothers cartoon.

I always felt like something was wrong with me because I had to leave class every day after lunch for speech therapy sessions. At the time, I had only been training in the martial arts for a few years. My father, who was also my martial arts instructor, said something to me that changed the way I viewed my speech challenge. He said, "You are very fortunate to have your own private speech coach. You have the opportunity to learn to become a great speaker."

My father's powerful words gave me the resilience to weather the verbal bullying and overcome my stuttering. They instilled in me the "never give up" and "yes, I can" attitude that comes with being a martial artist. His words gave me the confidence to eventually become a recognized speaker in the martial arts industry.

As a kid, I grew up in a tough neighborhood in the Mission District of San Francisco. My family owned one of the better-known

Karate schools in the city. We had a big yellow light box sign on the side of our building that featured our last name in three-foot-tall letters. Because of our notoriety bullies would challenge me regularly. I always knew it was going down when the opening line was, "So you're that Beliso kid, huh? Let's see some of that Karate stuff." Practicing the martial arts and being able to defend myself saved my life many times over.

Then one sad day, my good friend and martial arts classmate Carlo Del Castillo, was shot and killed at the age of fifteen. He was one of the best fighters I knew in and out of the ring, but even he couldn't stop a bullet. The cold reality of Carlo's death taught me that you can't fight all the time and the best fight was the one you never got into.

From the age of eight until seventeen, I trained six days a week, four hours a day, and competed in tournaments every other weekend. During this time, martial arts was my life. I literally ate, slept and drank it twenty-four seven. As my trainer, my father told me how much to eat, how much to weigh, how many kicks and punches to throw, and how to fight in the ring.

One Friday night we were getting in some extra work for a tournament the next day. I looked at my father and said, "Dad, it's 9:30 p.m.—how much more can we train?" He clenched his jaw and cleared his throat as he always did before he was about to say something of great importance.

"When you are not training, the other guy is, and he will be the one to beat you tomorrow," my father answered. He trained me well past 11:00 p.m. that night.

The next day I took first place at the California Karate Championships in both forms and sparring. I went on to win over one hundred major tournaments during my competitive years. What I learned from this way of thinking and training was that if you want to succeed, you have to be willing to work harder than everyone else. It nurtured a kind of work ethic that has helped me to succeed with several businesses and careers.

At the age of twenty, I stopped competing to pursue a career in music. Over the next ten years, I played in bands and clubs on the local music scene. I eventually went solo and signed a record deal overseas in the Philippines. I had a number one song and toured extensively.

Through all of this I continued to practice martial arts. The heat and pollution were so bad where I lived that I had to train after 11:00 p.m. My workout—which consisted of running, shadowboxing, calisthenics, and practicing forms—kept me company well into the midnight hour. Meditation rounded out my nightly training as a reminder that the martial arts are my life. Being involved in martial arts was the one thing that kept me grounded and focused through all the craziness that went with a rock-and-roll lifestyle.

After touring and promoting my album for three years, I returned home to San Francisco. I had tasted fame and fortune but decided to give it up. Something was missing in my life, and I felt like I lacked purpose. I went back to my first love, which was teaching the martial arts. I offered classes in several different dojos and health clubs, and then I decided to open my own school with a little help from friends who believed in me.

Martial arts gave me the life I live today. Through the opportunities and challenges of growing this business, I learned that my purpose is to serve people and affect change in the martial arts industry. I created a successful business model based upon service, not selling. I have a vision that we as martial artists and school owners can better serve our communities if we put people before profits as opposed to behaving like used-car salesmen trying to close a deal. I have committed myself to this movement by sharing my message with school owners and businesses throughout the world.

I have had a love affair with the martial arts for over fifty years. It has been the one constant in my life that has been there to pick me up, steer me in the right direction, and challenge me to be a better person. The martial arts have given me the purpose to help people live their best life through service.

I am dedicated to mastering myself through practicing the martial arts because martial arts have saved my life, are my life, and gives me life.

Brannon Beliso is an eighth-degree black belt, a former recording artist with three top ten hits, the owner of two very successful schools in the martial arts industry, and the creator of an internationally distributed life-skills education system. Brannon is an established author, writer, speaker, consultant, teacher and mentor.
www.BrannonBeliso.com

"And Now . . . About My Love Life"

Kevin Bourke

It amounted to the perfect storm. My marriage of nearly twenty years was ending; I had recently left the religion of my youth, causing much of my family to excommunicate me; and the economy was tanking—which, as a financial adviser, affected my livelihood in a most significant way.

All of this happened in 2008, the year of the mortgage meltdown and the greatest recession since the Depression. Lehman Brothers and other financial institutions collapsed, millions of people lost their jobs, and the financial future of the entire nation seemed to be hanging on a precipice.

Earning my black belt in martial arts was the one thing that gave me the focus and confidence to make it through this dark passage. My training began in 2006, and I steadily worked my way up through the ranks, earning different colored belts, each indicating a new level of skill.

As luck would have it, 2008 and 2009—the darkest years for me personally and for the nation economically—coincided with the most challenging portion of my martial arts career: being a black belt candidate. A black belt candidate is a person who has earned all the lower ranking belts and is honing his or her art in preparation for the black belt test.

As a candidate, I knew I not only would be expected to have all that I'd learned assimilated into my person (which goes way beyond memorizing), but also be able to display my skills in front of a large audience. A portion of the test involves actually defending oneself against attackers—at one point, three attackers at once. All of the years spent training on the mat, watching videos of martial arts instructors and fighters, mentally reviewing defense, kicks, throwforms, takedowns, practicing with other students and Senseis—all of it came down to this intense, demanding period prior to the actual test.

During those early days after my separation and subsequent divorce when I'd find myself despondent, the energy, focus, and determination that being a black belt candidate demanded kept me putting one foot in front of the other.

When much of my family, including my father, stopped all communication with me due to their religious beliefs, the family of friends I made through martial arts gave me community.

My financial advisory business during those dark days suffered as you might imagine. More importantly, hundreds of client families relied on me through those difficult times to offer guidance and perspective. One of the tenets in our dojo, indomitable spirit, reminded me that all was not lost, this too shall pass, and I just had to keep going.

Now, about my love life.

If you're old enough, you'll remember those old ads in the back of magazines showing a young man and his girlfriend at the beach. A bully kicks sand in the young man's face. Yeah, that was me. For the young man in the ad, the solution was Charles Atlas' bodybuilding course. For me, it was martial arts. It wasn't that I ever experienced anyone kicking sand in my face, but I always felt intimidated. Martial arts taught me to leave that behind. At the same time, our dojo emphasizes the tenet of courtesy, which precludes a martial artist from acting in a cocky manner. I experienced a level of confidence in dealing with the opposite sex that had previously evaded me.

After earning my black belt, one of my fellow black belts invited me to her birthday party in a nearby town. I pulled up in front of her house, noticed a very attractive woman parking across the street from me, and thought, *I hope she's going to the same party I am.* She was—and we're still together six years later. Later we learned that someone at that party saw us talking and said, "Seeing them is like watching popcorn pop"—an apt description, and one I love.

Martial arts introduced me to the fellow student, who in turn introduced me to the love of my life. But perhaps just as important, martial arts gave me the confidence to speak to a beautiful woman who, just months before, might have intimidated me.

As for business? Well, the mortgage crisis came and went, but my business has flourished. Partially it has to do with another tenet we practice at our dojo—integrity—which I attempt to incorporate into every relationship. But it was the tenet of perseverance that gave me the impetus to keep going when so many financial advisers left the industry completely. I see where my business is today, and I am thankful every moment that I stayed the course.

One might not think that martial arts would help a person build a financial advisory business, but earning my black belt was one of the core factors in my success.

Today I wonder where I would have been if martial arts hadn't entered my life. This discipline gave me friends when I had very few, a life partner when I had none, the confidence to build a successful business, and physical fitness as the final reward.

What has martial arts meant to me? As it turns out, everything.

Kevin Bourke is the author of the book Make Your Money Last a Lifetime *and founder of Bourke Wealth Management. Since 1987 he has worked as a financial advisor helping investors reach their goals. Kevin has two beautiful daughters, Olivia and Rachael, and lives in Santa Barbara, California.*

www.bourkewealth.com

How My Biggest Failure Launched My Career

Erica L. Martin

I'll never forget the overwhelming feeling of anxiety and nervousness that washed over me as I stepped up to the podium to make my first public speech.

I was eighteen years old, and this was the biggest moment of my life. The auditorium was filled with parents and kids who had come for the grand opening of my new martial arts school. The pressure was on, all eyes were on me, and if felt as if time slowed down as I walked from my seat to the front of the room.

I would love to tell you that I rose to the occasion and delivered an eloquent speech that dazzled the audience and left them both impressed and inspired, but that would be a lie. I totally bombed.

It was the biggest moment of my life, and I couldn't possibly have crashed and burned in a more glorious fashion. I stumbled on my words. I repeated, "Uh, I'm just really thankful for this opportunity . . ." ad nauseam. I flushed bright red and nervous-laughed my way down into awkward speech history.

It was the longest five minutes of my life.

I fought back tears as I sat down in my chair, embarrassed and feeling the soul-crushing despair of public failure. I silently questioned, "Am I even good enough to have my own school? Will I ever be able to inspire people and transform the lives of kids and families in my local community? Will I ever be able to face anyone ever again?"

Suddenly my mental pity party was interrupted because I had to get out on the floor and perform a martial arts demonstration. Thank goodness, *this* was something I knew I could do!

My techniques were crisp and strong and complimented by smooth, flowing circular movements. My eyes were laser-focused, and intensity radiated from my body. I channeled all the fear, nervousness, disappointment, and embarrassment into an intense, inspiring, and flawless martial arts demonstration befitting a well-trained black belt.

As the crowd roared with applause and admiration, I instantly knew what I had to do. I had to practice my public speaking the same way I practiced martial arts. I had to push myself out of my comfort zone, put on my proverbial white belt, and dedicate myself to the practice of becoming an inspiring speaker.

I started small by speaking at the end of my kids' classes and giving a little mini speech about how to have good character and how to be a leader in life. The kids and parents loved it, and it was a great confidence builder for me! Then I started doing the same thing with my adult classes (which was an easy little step since most of my adult students were parents of the kids in my earlier class). I modified the message for my adult students, shared my personal experiences, and surprisingly they loved it, too!

As my confidence with public speaking grew, I began reaching out to local elementary schools to see if there was a way I could spread the messages I was teaching in my school to empower and inspire their students. When they said yes, I knew this was my chance to start inspiring positive change in a big way. I also knew this was my first real opportunity to rewrite the "script" in my head that said I was a failure at public speaking.

I approached each of these school talks with the discipline I applied to my martial arts training. I practiced my talking points and my cadence; I made sure my message was clear, concise, and powerful. I visualized myself standing in front of the crowd, smiling confidently, and speaking clearly. I visualized thunderous applause and cheering that came from students, teachers, and parents alike.

As prepared as I was, when it came time for my first talk at the elementary school, I still felt scared, anxious, and nervous. I stared down the barrel of a microphone in front of eight hundred-plus students, teachers, and parents, but this time my training kicked in!

I took a deep breath and delivered my message, just the way I had practiced. I smiled confidently, made eye contact with the members of my audience, and my fear and nervousness melted away. Much to my surprise, the most amazing thing happened at the end . . .

As I wrapped up and thanked the audience, I heard a noise that started from the back and began echoing louder and louder throughout the room. It was the thunderous applause and cheering I had visualized, but this time it was in real life!

From there I continued to speak on bigger and bigger stages, and each time I would go through the same routine of visualizing and practicing, the way I had been taught in my martial arts training. It was so fulfilling when people came up to me at the end of my talk to tell me how it inspired them to take action, or how it touched and moved them. Every time that happened, it reaffirmed that I was doing the work I was meant to do.

Over the years I've built a career around speaking and consulting. I've become a sought-after international speaker, and I travel across the country sharing my message and coaching other entrepreneurs. I feel so incredibly blessed to be able to live a life I love! I am able to enjoy traveling, financial freedom, and impacting thousands of lives—all because I chose to apply the same formula to public speaking that I had learned as a black belt in the martial arts.

Erica L. Martin is an international speaker and successful entrepreneur, having built several multiple six-figure businesses. Her passion is teaching others the mindset and strategies necessary to build their dream business and live a life they love. Wakeboarding, sunset beach walks, and salsa dancing are some of Erica's favorite ways to recharge.

www.ericalmartin.com

Sometimes Your Path Finds You

Roger Boggs

I was not born into a martial arts family. When I graduated from college, I didn't say, "Man, I should open up a Karate school." I think sometimes your path finds you. I'd like to share the story of how my path found me.

The year was 1995. My son was thirteen years old and lashing out at the world. He had started to fight in school, and at home he "dug his heels in the sand." Not only did he defy anything his mom and I requested, he would actually do the opposite.

In my youth I was fortunate enough to grow up behind the YMCA in Cedar Rapids, Iowa, where I was given a scholarship to use the facility. There I trained in boxing, wrestling, and Taekwondo. Now I figured that if my son was going to fight, I had better teach him how.

I thought it was best to search for an outside source to help my son, so I looked in the phone book and called the closest Karate school near our home. When I walked in the dojo, I met Mike Anderson of Goshin Karate & Judo Academy. I told him I had done some Taekwondo and wrestling as a kid. He informed me that Karate was like Taekwondo and Judo was like wrestling.

My first response was, "Wow, you teach both arts at the same place?" You see, Goshin was offering mixed martial arts before MMA was cool.

I enrolled my son, and after a couple of months, I decided that I should get up off the couch and start training too. After all, I didn't want my son to be able to kick my butt someday!

Well, long story short, my son retired from martial arts training after obtaining his brown belt, which was a great achievement for a fifteen-year-old boy, considering that cars and girls were more important to him. I, however, achieved my black belt in 2000 and continued to practice at Goshin. Then in 2006 an interesting chain of events changed my life forever.

I walked into the dojo one day, and Mike Anderson said, "The dojo is for sale! I am either selling it or closing it." Coincidently, my real estate partnership was moving in a direction I didn't agree with, and I was looking for other opportunities. I set up a meeting with Mr. and Mrs. Anderson the very next day to purchase the dojo. I was honored and excited to continue Goshin's legacy.

And that brings me to where I am today. Goshin Karate & Judo Academy is primarily a youth-based martial arts learning center that focuses on life skills, self-defense, fitness, and fun.

Over the last ten years, we have faced our challenges like every other martial arts school and have always managed to overcome them. We have created a great team of adult and teen black belt instructors.

I love martial arts. And most of all, I love being a teacher— a teacher of teachers. A martial arts teacher is many things: a mother figure, a father figure, a coach, a caretaker, a nurse, a doctor, a babysitter, a life coach, a nutritionist, a therapist, a friend, a motivator, a cheerleader, a motivational speaker, a teacher, a role model, and a mentor. I wouldn't have it any other way!

For me, this is the greatest life I could ever have. I wasn't looking for this path—it found me!

I especially enjoy sharing my love and passion for the martial arts with kids—they keep me young, and I get to help them achieve their best. I feel very fortunate to be there when that little lightbulb goes off. With them, I'm something like a game show host, a stand-up comedian, a lounge singer, a dad, a vaudeville juggler, and a play-by-play commentator.

It's a privilege to interact with students who have good hearts and do what's expected of them. Seeing them grow up into good, thoughtful adults is my best reward. And on those rare occasions when they come back for a visit, it is always a joyful reunion. I feel even more blessed when my students grow up and bring *their* kids to Goshin. It is a real privilege to be a part of people's lives this way.

I keep a John C. Maxwell quote taped to my computer monitor that keeps me on my path: "People do not care how much you know until you show them how much you care."

Oh, and by the way, my son grew up to be an awesome young man. He has become an excellent father and has given this old sensei five grandkids. Maybe a similar path will find one of them and inspire them to carry on my passion.

Roger Boggs is a man of action. He shares an exciting message of optimism and believes he can make a difference in the world by empowering the youth in his community to be leaders and everyday heroes. He prides himself as a teacher, life coach, motivational speaker, business owner, songwriter, husband, father, and grandpa.

www.GoshinKarate.com

Power from Compassion

Austin Curtis

The sun had just set beautifully behind the evergreens, and it was beginning to get dark. A few college buddies and I sat next to a crackling campfire, enjoying a cliff-side view of Western Alberta. It was our first time off campus together, and it felt good to be free from the strict rules of the dorms.

I don't remember exactly what we were joking about, but I distinctly remember the moment that I stopped laughing. One of my buddies—I'll call him Jesse—stood up with a beer in his hand and rather cheerfully announced that his girlfriend had just dumped him and he had decided to kill himself. There was a split second of silence, and then an uncomfortable burst of laughter from the group. "Sit down and shut up," someone heckled. Seemingly content with his announcement, Jesse took the last sip of his beer and stumbled off toward the trees.

After sitting there for another minute, I realized that I was the only one sober enough to take Jesse seriously. I got up from the fire and hurried to catch up to him. My eyes squinted as I adjusted to the dim light of the half moon. I made my way past a few rows of trees and found him sitting on the edge where the side of the cliff began sloping downward. I sat down and talked with him for a few minutes, doing my best to console him. Once I understood that nothing I was saying was making a difference, I switched to a more serious tone and told him that I was taking him back with me. He jumped up at this and began sliding down the slope into the darkness, ignoring my shouts to stop. "I'll jump with you," I heard myself yell out. "Wait for me!"

I slid down cautiously on the loose ground and stopped once I could see him again. He was just steps away from a two-hundred-foot drop with a desperate smile on his face pointing down to the rocky creek below. He said something about jumping down as I cautiously made my way closer to him. When I was within reach, I felt a surge of adrenaline and decisiveness shoot through me. Instinctively I used a takedown from my years of martial arts training and pinned him to the ground. From this position I talked to him until he understood that I was ready to do anything to keep him from jumping off that cliff—even if it meant knocking him out cold and carrying him back with me. After a few escape attempts on his part, I managed to get him back to the campsite, where he eventually passed out.

That night was the first time that I had ever used my martial arts skills outside of the dojo, and it was a life-altering experience for me. I didn't feel like a hero—I just felt thankful that we all made it back to campus. Over the next few months, the result was a transformation in my belief about where my source of power and strength came from.

That surge of adrenaline was more than anything I had experienced in sports or even in my martial arts training. It felt like I was operating at the peak of my physical potential in terms of power, speed, and clarity of mind.

Before that night, I had only ever experienced something similar when I was intensely angry—like the time I chased my brother through the house and tackled him to the ground for embarrassing me in front of my friends. Or the time I found out that my parents were splitting up and nearly ripped a tree out of the ground. I felt superhuman in those moments, so naturally I came into the belief that I had to be angry in order to tap into my highest level of strength.

The experience on the cliff changed all of that because I had tapped into that energy without anger. The power that came from my compassion was just as powerful—the biggest difference being my ability to see what was actually going on. I now believe that anger has only clouded my vision and kept me in a dark state of mind, whereas compassion gave me clarity and understanding, letting the light in.

In no way have I figured it all out, but one thing I can say is that I believe that my martial arts training has given me a sense of duty to protect those around me and the ability to operate at my highest physical and mental capacity from a place of compassion.

Austin Curtis is a fifth degree master instructor at his school, Martial Arts Family Fitness, in Santa Barbara, California. Austin also enjoys photography with his wife, Dara, and playing with their three beautiful daughters on the beach in Carpinteria.

www.kickboxers.com

Training from the Inside Out

Benny "The Jet" Urquidez

"Why does he talk like that?"

My brother slapped me across the head and said, "Ah, don't be disrespectful."

I was thirteen, attending a martial arts demonstration, and it was the first time I had ever heard anybody with that kind of accent. The man was from Hong Kong; his name was Bruce Lee.

It was 1965, and Bruce Lee was talking about his "four-finger punch" and how to use internal power. Standing next to him was a 250-pound gentleman with a big weight-lifting plate held up in front of his chest. Bruce put four fingers to the plate and then hit it—driving the guy backward three feet into the air and knocking him across the room. I immediately jumped up and said, "I want to do that!"

I had already been fighting for a while. Actually, while all the neighborhood kids had toy trucks, I had boxing gloves. I was boxing at the age of three and competing in the 1958 Boxing Peewee Division when I was six. A year later I started competing in Judo until 1963, when I started Kenpo Karate.

However, witnessing that Bruce Lee demonstration really made me want to understand the martial arts at a deeper level. My mother had always talked to me about internal power, but until that moment, I had no idea what she was talking about.

My mother was a professional wrestler, and she was always trying to provide me with insight and internal understanding. For instance, when I would sit with my father while he watched boxing on TV, he would slap me and say, "Look at that!" I would turn to him and say, "Okay, I'm watching." And then I would go in the kitchen and my mother would hug me and explain that he didn't know how to verbally say it, but that was how he showed his love for me.

She taught me how to work with emotion, the frequency of thought, and the power of words. I learned to integrate these teachings with the physical demands of martial arts training.

I got my first black belt at the age of fourteen and began competing against men twice my size and twice my weight. I knew I had to continue to get my strength from the inside out.

In 1973 I was invited to compete in Hawaii at the first Martial Arts World Championship. Imagine a Mixed Martial Arts elimination tournament with no weight divisions and no rules whatsoever. At 5'6" and 145 pounds, I won the championship, beating Dana Goodson, who was 6'3" and 225 pounds.

The beautiful thing about training in the martial arts is that it puts a threat in front of you. And when a threat is in front of you, all the emotions you hide under your bed or hide in your closet come to the surface. I learned that if you want to change how you feel, you have to change your thoughts.

I became really good at acting under pressure, especially when it came to street fighting. A lot of people would challenge me because I was small, so I had a lot of opportunity to understand the emotions and gain the mental edge because of this training. Yes, I had several black belts in different systems, but it was the mental edge I developed that made my opponents so frustrated and upset at me. When I fought, I wasn't thinking about winning. I was just having fun.

I would smile, and they would say, "I'm going to knock that smile off your face," and I just kept on smiling. I was thankful for them, because without them I couldn't do what I loved doing. I was grateful they were in front of me.

Since retiring from professional fighting, I've been helping people with this idea and teaching them how they can reprogram their thoughts. I tell them, "If you don't like the way you feel, change the way you think."

The brain needs three things:

1. The brain needs to focus on what you want, so that your soul can manifest it.
2. The brain needs a hero or mentor so you can take the best things from them and make them yours.
3. The brain needs mantras to tell yourself that you are worthy of happiness. (This is important because if you don't feel worthy, you sabotage yourself.)

Remember, if you don't like the way you feel, change the way you think. That's exactly what I do.

One of my favorite movie projects was *Road House* with Patrick Swayze. I was his trainer and stunt double. Nobody could ever call that work—it was so much fun.

One day we were doing a fight scene that I was choreographing, and Patrick was getting very frustrated. "I'm a dancer—why can't I find the rhythm of this?" He was also a great martial artist, but it wasn't working for him. He was stuck in his head. I told him, "It's okay, I know where we have to go with this."

The next day when I went to his home studio, I could see the dread in his eyes as he thought, *Oh, here we go again.*

I said, "Patrick, watch this."

I put on some music, and I started dancing with martial arts movement. I could see Patrick's foot start tapping on the ground. His shoulders began moving with me, and he started getting into what I was doing. He jumped up and started dancing with me and I said, "Okay, now add this technique."

Within five minutes he had the fight choreography down. He could relate to the music, and it changed how he thought about it. In fact, Patrick got so excited about the fight scenes that after that he was the first one on set to get started in the morning.

Life is a roller-coaster ride of emotions, up and down, and taking one day at a time is what it is all about. Learning to train yourself from the inside out is mastery. We all have that internal power. Sometimes we just need to forget what we know and remember what we have forgotten.

Benny "The Jet" Urquidez, martial arts master, actor, and fight choreographer, is one of the most famous martial artists in the world. Sensei Benny retired from professional competition after remaining undefeated for twenty-seven years—he is the longest reigning World Champion in history, not just across all weight classes and in all styles of martial arts, but in any sport on earth.
www.bennythejet.com

Practicing Martial Arts at the Salon

Fay Doe

As the plane bumped up and down, the turbulence kept coming in bigger waves. A voice came over the loudspeaker: "This is the captain speaking. We are experiencing a moderate amount of turbulence; please keep your seatbelt fastened." *Moderate?* Who was he kidding?

Although flying is not my favorite thing, I've had to do a lot of it over the years to visit family in the UK. And of all the times I've done this trip, I can tell you, this was *not* moderate. It was extreme.

I was traveling by myself to be with my mum, as my step-father had just passed away. I was already in an emotional state of mind, and each bout of turbulence was driving me further over the edge . . .

Then I remembered to breathe. I started taking deep, focused breaths like we practiced in my Hapkido class. (I think one of my fellow travelers thought I was going to have a baby!) I remembered what I had been taught: that I needed to be calm and to still my mind. I had learned that I could breathe through anything.

After a while the turbulence passed, and I was able to breathe normally again. I was struck by just how much my study of Hapkido and becoming a Black Belt had influenced my life outside of the dojo.

Growing up in a large family on the south coast of England, I was not able to do the same things other kids did. We were poor, so I didn't take swim lessons or learn how to ride a bike. I had early-age rheumatism, inherited from my father, that usually kept me off to the side on the playground or inside the classroom during physical education classes. In those days, we didn't know how to treat rheumatism other than aspirin, Tiger Balm, and hot water bottles when I would wake up in pain at night.

I firmly believed I was not a "physical type of person."

When I chose to become a hairdresser, everyone was skeptical that I would be able to do it. "You'll never be able to stand up all day," they said. Determined to prove them wrong and with a passion for the craft of hairdressing and beauty, I soon showed them otherwise.

After my first visit to my family in California (paid for and encouraged by my brother Bob), I realized I could live some-place where my joints wouldn't hurt all the time. I felt "lighter," and I enjoyed the lifestyle.

I spent several years building my salon in Santa Barbara, and then one day I looked in the mirror to find that I had gained weight. I had been focusing on my business and not on myself.

It was time to do something, so I cautiously entered Martial Arts Family Fitness that had recently opened in Santa Barbara. I wore my fattest sweats (I did not want to be mistaken for someone who worked out), and after the first resistance bands class (which I enjoyed, much to my surprise), I signed up for more. I began kickboxing a few weeks later and was pleasantly surprised when some of the "fit" people in class asked me to join them for coffee after class.

I continued to work out and feel better. I started watching the martial artists at the school, and after a year I felt confident enough to start my own black-belt journey.

I am now a second dan Black Belt, having studied under Grand Master Wheaton for several years. The things I have learned have helped me in my life pretty much every day.

I practice my martial arts at my salon. When I think I am tired, I "dig deep," just like on the mat at the dojo.

When I am challenged, I breathe through it and come out the other side.

The thing I practice daily is "perfect practice." Grand Master Wheaton explains it as the way to constantly become better at what one is doing. I have passed that on to my trainees and my staff as a lifelong practice.

There are many great things about studying to become a Black Belt, but knowing I can work hard, achieving a goal and seeing it to the end, is probably one of the biggest lessons. It doesn't matter what anyone else says or thinks—I now know I can do it.

Fay Doe is the owner and creative director of Underground Hair Artists, voted one of the Top 200 Salons in America. Fay is an entrepreneur, hairstylist, and industry educator. She created Underground Culture, a natural, botanical haircare line that donates one dollar of each product sale to youth music and arts programs.

www.undergroundhairartists.com

What Wouldn't Have Been

Michael Mershad

Parents and students look at all I have accomplished and assume that I am a natural martial artist. However, as a short, skinny twelve-year-old boy with very little flexibility, I was not the toughest student in the adult program of my Taekwondo school all those years ago.

I remember the frustration of wanting to be better than the other students, wanting to hold my own in my class. As a Yellow Belt, only three months into my training, I told my parents I wanted to quit. I was not a natural martial artist, and even worse, I wasn't allowed to test for my next belt because I was short a few classes.

My dad sat down with me and told me that if he allowed me to quit martial arts so early in my journey, I would be quitting things for the rest of my life. He went on to incentivize me by purchasing a Sega Genesis® gaming system if I promised to stay with the program for at least a year without complaining. (I think it was the first—and maybe the only—time that video games motivated someone to stay in martial arts.)

That talk literally changed the trajectory of my life and thousands of others through the years.

After deciding that I would stick it out with martial arts, the next hurdle in my journey was being competent at sparring. Learning forms was never really an issue for me, but due to my size and the fact that I was in a class with adults, sparring posed a challenge. Back when I was a beginner, no one ever taught me how to spar. We were simply told to get a partner, bow, and spar. We were supposed to learn through trial and error.

A few months into sparring, my dad again told me something that solidified the man that I became. After watching me spar in class one night, he took me out to dinner. As we sat there, he said, "Mike, you know that you aren't the biggest student in class. You also know that you aren't as experienced as most of the students you sparred with tonight. One thing that I noticed about you, though, is that you never back down. No matter how hard you get hit or how much faster or more flexible the other students are, you never back down. I'm proud of you. Keep that up, and you'll be great at this and anything else you put your mind to."

We all have the ability to believe or disregard things that are said to us. If someone calls you stupid or says that you are terrible at something, you can choose to believe that—and therefore imprint that on your personal view of your identity. Or you can erase that from your memory altogether. You have the ability to do the same thing when a compliment is extended to you.

Since that meal with my dad, I have been someone who doesn't back down. It is ingrained into my identity and into my view of myself. When I face adversity, when I want to quit, when I get down on myself in any way, I mentally revert to that mind-set: I am Michael Mershad, and I don't back down!

I switched martial arts schools six months before my black belt testing because of a move to Atlanta. There I was introduced to the modern and motivational teaching style of Master Lowell Starr.

Mr. Starr took me under his wing—and took my training to the next level. I met my next training challenge: board breaking. I had never broken boards before, and I was required to do so in order to pass my upcoming belt testing as well as every future testing.

My initial inconsistent attempts were due to a mental struggle rather than a physical challenge. Mr. Starr, however, offered this advice as he worked to help me break more consistently. "Repetition and muscle memory," he said, "are the keys to breaking. There is no shortcut. If you are willing to put in the extra time that it takes to hone each move, then you will be able break whatever you want, whenever you want."

That motivational lesson has stuck with me not only for breaking boards, but for anything I want to improve upon. From public speaking to jump spin kicks, I put in the time that most are unwilling to devote so I can rise to a level that few will ever experience.

Over the next several years, I had many personal break-throughs, including earning my black belt, becoming an instructor, and opening my own academy in the Dayton, Ohio, area. I marvel at the life I now have and the number of things I never would have been able to do or experience had my parents allowed me to quit all of those years ago.

I never would have been the men's fourth degree world champion in 2002. I never would have won titles in X-Treme form competitions. I never would have had the chance to see three of my daughters, as well as my amazing wife, earn their black belts. My youngest daughter is on track to earn her black belt in 2019. I never would have had an article written about me in *Tae-kwondo Times* magazine or been asked to speak on the world stage at the Martial Arts SuperShow in Las Vegas in 2016.

All those experiences and countless others would have never happened if I had quit. Most importantly, however, is the fact that I never would have been able to inspire and develop thousands of students over the years, including my amazing staff and instructor team members. I am humbled and honored to have the opportunity to continue serving students and their families on a daily basis.

Sometimes there are days when I question my impact and the direction I am going. On those days, I remind myself: "I am Michael Mershad, and I don't back down!"

Michael Mershad is a seventh degree Black Belt in Taekwondo and has a passion for working with other school owners and students, helping them to make giant leaps in their own lives. His mission is to provide martial arts leaders with strategic vision, training, and resources to keep their programs relevant and effective into the next generation.
  www.MichaelMershad.com

Visualize to Optimize

Bill Keiran

About ten years ago, when I was preparing for my second dan test in Hapkido, something happened that completely changed the way I train, as well as the way I face other trials in my life.

It was spring break, so my family and I headed out for a week to the mountains. As the weather would have it, we received about a foot of fresh snow overnight, so off to the slopes we went. My wife and daughter were going to go skiing; my son and I were going snowboarding.

Now, I'm an active, healthy, and fit early-forties kinda guy. But here's the thing: I'd never snowboarded before . . . ever.

Within a couple hours my son and I were feeling pretty good, maybe even a little cocky. I had waterskied for years, which is almost the same thing, right? I decided it was time to head for higher ground. My son decided to hang out a little lower. Up I went.

It wasn't until I really started to pick up some speed coming down the mountain that it hit me: *What the hell was I thinking?* It was steep, and I was going fast. As I approached the lower portion of the slope, I saw out of the corner of my left eye someone coming right toward me. Of course, he had his back to me and couldn't see me, but I could see him.

Quicker than a snap of a finger, I decided to cut sharply to the left, and that's when it happened. My board caught an edge, and over I went—*hard*. So hard that my left shoulder slammed through the twenty-four-inch hard pack. All I heard was a snap, crackle, and pop. All I saw were stars.

And then the strangest thing happened.

I calmly stood up and grabbed my board as my two kids ran over and asked if I was OK. I said, "No" (calmly, of course), and I asked them to take my board and have their mother meet me in the Med Tent.

I walked over, stepped inside, and announced that I had just crashed and broke something.

Everyone was a bit surprised at my calmness. Even more amazing was my pulse, which was around sixty-five. No one could believe it, but I was controlling my breath and visualizing by focusing on a point within me to calm things down.

Breathing and visualizing. I hadn't really understood the power of either technique until that day. Sure, I knew what each meant. My martial arts teacher, Grandmaster Wheaton, instructed us use breathing as a way to warm up in class, and he talked to us about visualizing during certain moves. But now it finally came full circle, and I understood *why* he had us do those breathing and visualization exercises. Both had kicked in subconsciously.

X-rays revealed that I had three breaks at the collarbone/shoulder and one upper arm fracture. My doctor said I'd be looking at three months minimum to get back to training. All I could think was, *How am I going to be ready for my test?* At best I would only have about six weeks to prepare. And for the style of Hapkido I study, that was not a lot of time.

Several people said, "Why not wait for the next test date?" But I had trained too hard and too long to wait another year. I knew that as long as I let my body heal, I'd find a way. So that's when and where I took Grandmaster's teaching of visualization to the max.

I began my "visualize to optimize" mantra. I showed up to classes. I didn't just watch the class, I visualized myself in the class. I also made the conscious decision to spend a minimum of fifteen minutes each day visualizing some part of my training—every technique, every stance, every strike, every weapon. I made myself visualize it all. Sometimes I visualized the entire test in my head in one session.

Another beautiful thing that happened: Grandmaster constantly checked in with me. He believed I could pull it together, and he wasn't giving me an out. It was as though he believed I could make this happen, and he was waiting for me to "see" it, too.

The day finally came when I could get back on the mat. Physically I had needed time away, but mentally it felt as though I had never stopped training. Everything I had seen and done in my mind began to take shape on the mat. I was ready . . .

I tested on schedule, and it felt awesome. It may have been my best test ever. I know with certainty that the visualization that I practiced all those months—and still do to this day—optimized the success of that test . . . and every test since.

While I'm not a religious person, from a spiritual perspective I feel that we are all meant to go through certain challenges while on this crazy ride through life. And for me, this was one of those challenges that made me stronger and taught me what I needed to learn.

I have used this strategy in many other areas of my life. I believe that if the mind is trained as equally as the body is trained, the body will do as the mind has done. See it, then be it.

That strike you visualize a thousand times will be that much sharper. That speech you visualize a thousand times will be that much smoother. That job interview you visualize will be that much more successful. Whatever it is, visualize it. Over and over and over—until it becomes not just what you do, but who you are.

Visualize what is to be—to optimize what will be.

Bill Keiran is happily married to his wife of twenty-eight years, Cindy, and operates his own successful HVAC business in Santa Barbara, California. A father of two, Bill has been training in martial arts for over twenty years. He is a fourth dan master instructor at Martial Arts Family Fitness and has several professional fitness certifications.
www.kickboxers.com

The Little Girl That Could

Melody Shuman

I'm five foot nothing, and I've never weighed a hundred pounds in my life; I can't even donate blood. Growing up so small, I wasn't the coolest person in school. As a matter of fact, when I walked into fifth grade at a new school, the cool girls said, "Who let the kindergartner in our class today?"

So . . . I might have wanted to stand out a little bit, and I might have had a little bit of an attitude . . . and my parents might have enrolled me in martial arts to help teach me some discipline—but that's another story.

When I started martial arts in 1987, things were very different than they are today. Kids and adults trained side by side, and we all tested on the same material for our belts, regardless of age. At first I hated it; I thought it was hokey. I thought the white outfits were cheesy and, as a petite eleven-year-old girl, training next to a big, sweaty man totally grossed me out.

Everything changed the day I put on sparring gear for the first time and kicked a boy in the head, really hard. That felt good—not kicking him in the head, but the fact that everybody was cheering! I thought, *This is awesome—you get to beat boys up and everybody cheers you on! I love this sport!*

I continued training and earned my black belt. However, when I was in high school, the other kids picked on me for being in martial arts, so I dropped out to play soccer for a while.

Ironically, martial arts came calling back to me. I got a job—my first job—because I was a Black Belt. Disney World hired me; I'm not supposed to say what I did, but let's just say I had a really cool job and being a Black Belt help me get that job. I got back into martial arts because I missed it, and I've never looked back.

Martial arts became a lifestyle, not just a sport or a hobby or a job.

When I was on the world demo team, we traveled to South Korea. We visited a martial arts school, and one of the masters asked me to teach class. I jumped out on the mat and suddenly realized that the students were preschoolers. *Uh-oh.*

Most martial arts schools avoid teaching this age group. The kids haven't yet developed good memory, discipline, balance, self-control, or teamwork skills.

"Line up!" I said. They didn't.

"Okay, let's make a formation." No one moved.

I looked over at the master. "Do they speak English?" I asked. He shook his head. *Oh, this is going to be harder than I thought.*

I pulled from my black belt training and my experience at Disney. I set up an obstacle course and got them to follow along. I did my best to entertain them and yet teach them some skills. An hour later, the kids were still fully engaged and having a blast.

I was so motivated that I hurried to a bookstore, purchased some books on children and parenting, and spent the eighteen-hour flight from Seoul to Chicago reading, studying, and writing an entirely new curriculum for my school. I reverse-engineered the program. Instead of trying to teach martial arts and hoping my students would build skills, I found out what skills they were building at their stage of development—and then plugged in the martial arts activities using "edutainment."

As I implemented the new program, my school grew. I continued to study the way kids learn. What I discovered went against how most martial arts schools were training youthful students at the time. I also discovered that martial arts programs could be one of the most effective tools for helping children grow as a whole, more so than any other sport or activity.

Fast-forward to today. I've had the privilege of influencing thousands of school owners and instructors to rethink the way they teach children. I travel globally to speak about this new approach and how it improves a student's ability to learn and grow.

I never wake up and say, "Oh, I don't want to work today," or "I don't want to educate myself," or "I don't want to put time into my career," because I am passionate about what I do. And martial arts is the vehicle that my passion gets to use to motivate and inspire others.

Melody Shuman, a master martial arts instructor and successful entrepreneur, is the founder and creator of SKILLZ, an innovative, age-specific curriculum and teaching system used in hundreds of martial arts schools around the world. Melody lives with her family in St. Petersburg, Florida.

www.skillzworldwide.com

Managing Art Director

Frank Troise

Many martial arts articles talk about the "martial" of the art. Instead, I want to talk about the "art"—art in the simplest context.

One morning I was taking the bus to work. The bus was packed as commuters were sardined into this modern day "tin can."

These tin cans in Singapore are an example of cleanliness and discipline. Singapore is known for that, and disruptions to the pace and cadence are quite uncommon.

And so, in that quiet, cadenced sardine can, I grabbed the handle on the bus with my right hand as we slowly made our way downtown. Two work bags were between my legs.

All was quiet until we stopped at the next station. Suddenly I heard a passenger exploding down the aisle to be "first" out the door. Singaporeans are so elegant in their politeness, and no one said anything. Clearly he was not a local.

I had my back turned, so I couldn't see what was approaching. But I knew something was coming over my left shoulder. And it was coming fast.

Quickly the passenger hit my left arm to make his way through to the front. His motion was strong enough to seriously twist my arm.

But my training allowed me to leverage what I heard, and my arm was already ahead of his motion—in fact, it was retracting to hit him in the neck.

That was what I was trained to do. One shot. Done.

But as I slowly turned to face him and hit him accurately, I realized that I could seriously hurt him. From his eyes, he knew it, too.

I continued to turn my body to my left and retracted my arm down my left side, and didn't hit him at all.

But I did cause him to stop, and he decided to let everyone know that he was angry at what had almost happened.

The bus actually had come to a stop because of his loss of composure. I proceeded to do a quick check. My heart rate was fine, and my breathing was calm. My training once again kicked in, and I was steady.

So steady that I grabbed the two bags between my legs and held on in each hand; I was effectively "armless."

This passenger saw that I was vulnerable and decided to "call me out." I could tell he was not Singaporean, as this would never be allowed or tolerated. I knew my host country and respected its culture and people. Therefore I wasn't going to be drawn into this with him.

He continued to berate me.

Mind you, my wife was next to me as he verbally emasculated me fully in front of everyone.

Passengers were scared and began stepping back. Ironically a small space opened for us as he continued this one-sided bullying.

The doors on the bus behind him were open, and he indicated that he wanted me to step off the bus and settle this, one on one, man to man. He was loud and belligerent, but my heart rate remained steady; my breathing was controlled.

But I knew he needed to get off the bus because his presence was threatening to everyone. This bully was frightening my wife and my Singaporean colleagues.

I looked him square in the eye and could see that he was terrified. His breathing was frantic, and he was starting to perspire. And from my cold stare into his eyes he knew that I knew that.

I calmly put both bags down on the floor, slowly rolled up my sleeves, and turned to my wife: "I will meet you at the next bus stop in two minutes."

All of the passengers slowly exhaled as they heard what I was saying. Looking into his eyes, I could tell he realized that something had changed. His bullying was threatening everyone around me. Single moms. Elderly couples. Kids going to school. Very simply, I was not going to accept that. I needed him off the bus.

I checked my heart rate one last time. Steady. I checked my breathing. Calm.

I looked at him one last time, and he knew he was over. Over and done.

I turned to my wife and she looked up at me with the look of someone who knows with certainty what an outcome will be. She knew I would meet her at the next bus stop after I did what was required. I would meet her with my heart rate steady, my breathing calm, and she knew that I would be quick and efficient.

My wife looked me straight in my eyes and said, "You can do this."

I looked at her, nodded my head in agreement, and turned back to face my adversary.

He was gone—off the bus and gone. Just like that, he had disappeared.

The doors whooshed shut, I picked up my bags back in one hand, and grabbed the handle with the other.

Heart rate steady. Breathing calm.

Art.

Frank Troise is one of Asia's leading voices and practitioners on Fin-Tech. Mr. Troise is a frequent commentator on CNBC regarding market strategy and has over twenty years of experience managing multibillion-dollar portfolios. Mr. Troise's research, work, and career have been published in The Economist, Institutional Investor, The Wall Street Journal, *and other publications.*

www.FrankTroise.com

A Family Affair

Will Schneider

I don't remember a life without martial arts.

I began training when I was five years old. I was raised on Jean-Claude Van Damme, Steven Seagal, and Chuck Norris movies. It's all I can remember, and it's probably even intertwined in my DNA by now.

I first walked into the dojang with my father, William J. Schneider. It was August 1987, and we lived in the small town of London, Kentucky. Grandmaster Young Sun Kang was opening a new school, and it was still being built out. I remember seeing the tenets on the wall: courtesy, integrity, perseverance, self-control, indomitable spirit, and victory.

I loved training with my dad. He would ride his Harley-Davidson motorcycle to class with our gear bags and me on the back.

Martial arts soon became a passion for my entire family. Roughly a year after Dad and I began training, my mother, Victoria, and my oldest sister, Rachel, joined us on the mats. They too became Black Belts. Later my sisters Sarah, Anna, and Elizabeth joined the tradition, also achieving the black belt level. I honestly think my dad would've gotten the dogs involved too if it were possible.

Around our house there were always uniforms, safety gear, and belts; you can only imagine laundry day! I learned quickly how to use an ironing board.

In 1989 I became one of the youngest Black Belts at a time when it was definitely not typical. In fact, right after I received my black belt, my instructor told me to go change, and in the locker room was a brand-new assistant instructor uniform. Now that uniform popped!

Being a seven-year-old Black Belt meant I had to be the real deal. I had to train extra hard because sometimes bullies wanted to test me, and when I went to a tournament, I didn't want to embarrass my dad or my instructor.

The biggest life change for me, though, wasn't just receiving my own black belt—it was seeing my mother and four sisters receive theirs. And, on a side note, I can tell you I never worried about my sisters on date night!

Through the martial arts, I developed physical, social, and mental skills that have allowed me to live the life I'm blessed to live.

Physically I had the advantage of developing balance, coordination, and flexibility at a very young age.

Socially I met some of my closest friend through the martial arts, lifelong friends and mentors such as Dr. Kelly Meador, Charles Ruth, Grandmaster Jimmy Mc, Grandmaster Kirschbaum, Grandmaster Wes Ruiz, Mark Slane, Tracy Hensley, Jason Fultz, Chris Strack, Ben Robinson, and many more.

Mentally I learned invaluable life skills such as having a positive attitude, goal setting, leadership, time management, team building, mental fortitude, and focus.

If it hadn't been for the martial arts, my family and I would not be who we are today.

Through the martial arts I've been able to travel across the United States and visit other countries. I've met great friends, attended and hosted large tournaments (I even got a plaque from Mickey Mouse), became self-employed at twenty years old, and ran the London/Laurel County Family YMCA.

I definitely can say that all the hard, long hours of training paid off. There have been three highlights in my martial arts career so far: first, when I was inducted in the World Martial

Arts Hall of Fame at age fourteen; second, when I was given the keys to my first academy after I purchased it from my father; and third, when I completed my first degree black belt test in Krav Maga with black belt Harry Hunsucker in attendance.

A bonus highlight also comes to mind: the time I got to announce the World Champion winners at the Wide World of Sports Complex in Orlando, Florida. That was so much fun!

I still train in martial arts to keep my skills current and achieve new ranks. My training comes in handy both in the business world and for physical conditioning, not to mention self-defense should I ever need it.

For me the martial arts are most evident off the mat now that I'm a father. I am strong yet patient, orderly yet realistic with my kids.

Martial arts have made me a better father, a better leader for my students, a better brother to my family of black belts, and a better person who wants to enjoy life, always improve, help others, and leave a positive legacy in the world!

Master Will Schneider is a seventh degree Black Belt Master Instructor in Taekwondo, a fifth degree Master Instructor in Hapkido, and a second degree in Krav Maga. He was inducted in to the World Martial Arts Hall of Fame in 1996, and has been a columnist in many newspapers as well as Health Beat *magazine.*

www.EliteMa.org

The Girl with the Righteous Sword

Karina Munoz-Benalcazar

"She wasn't looking for a knight; she
was looking for a sword."

—*Atticus*

It was an exciting Friday night downtown, and everyone was out to party and have a good time. I was sitting at a bar with a girlfriend when a gentleman sat down next to us and started a conversation. When he said that he wanted to "take us home to continue the party," we told him we were not at all interested and asked him to leave. He stood up to go, and then unexpectedly leaned in as if to give us a hug. I was facing my friend and he was behind me. As he reached around to hug us good-bye, his hand came around in front of me, and he grabbed my breast.

It was as if a slow-motion film was playing as I instinctively grabbed his fingers and squeezed them as if milking a cow. I twisted them upward toward him so that his wrist was locked. As my focus on his hand became more intense, he began to yell, "Ouch, ouch, ouch, stop!"

I let go and stood up. There he was, a six-foot-tall predator. I turned to him and said, "Never do that. Never, ever to do that to any woman, ever." I pushed him back, knocking him into the wall, and walked away.

This was all quite alarming to my friend, who didn't fully understand what had happened. It must have looked quite strange to see her friend take on a man who was much bigger and over a foot taller.

I stand at four feet eleven and three-quarters inches tall. That three quarters of an inch is important because it allows me to round up to five feet tall. This may be meaningless to most, but for a short person, it matters. It all matters.

Growing up in a traditional Hispanic family, men were the valued warriors and helpers of women. I was taught that I was not to be loud or rude to men and never talk back. I was taught that I needed a knight to protect me, save me, and help me get through life.

I was also shorter than everyone, so even as an adult, many people couldn't help but look at me as a child. They would pick on me about various little things in my life and relationships. I always had to speak louder to be heard, get closer to be looked at, and sit at the same level in order to get my point across.

I also think that my height sometimes caused people to think of me as weaker, more vulnerable. For those who know me, that is not the case; if someone crosses me or I get angry about something I care about, the fiery, stereotypical Latina will come out in me. (Picture an angry Sophia Vergara on *Modern Family*, except in English.) However, in a dangerous situation where a life is threatened, it becomes a different story. Something more is needed—perhaps a knight in shining armor?

Well, I do not need a knight. I have a sword. My sword is martial arts. Martial arts taught me to use my voice. My voice truly matters. Martial arts taught me skills to defend myself. My skills allow me to feel confident in the world. Martial arts taught me how to be a knight.

I started in martial arts as an adult, but I was not immediately in love. I stuck with it because I had made a commitment.

It was not until I had been training for eight months that I saw what it was all about for me. During class my belt level finished basic techniques in the mirror, and the higher ranking belts continued with their basics while we watched. I suddenly saw my inspiration: a smaller, younger girl whose kicks were amazing. Her strong voice rang through the dojo, and her intensity and focus was incredible. She was only fourteen years old, and watching her made me never want to quit martial arts again until I could be her. To me, she was a knight—a female knight.

I decided to be a knight, too. I am so thankful I found martial arts. That "sword" is my life. I sharpen it physically and mentally all the time. It is internal and external. It is physical and intangible. I will always have it with me. I am never going to grow taller, but I will always be the small one with the strong sword.

I hope that everyone finds that sword. And I think it is especially important for women. Don't get me wrong—I hope we all find that knight, too. However, just think: Wouldn't it be cool that, if your knight is down, you could handle it all with your own righteous sword? #word

Karina Munoz-Benalcazar is a third-dan Black Belt in Dynamic Circle Hapkido. For over nine years she has been teaching students from ages three to sixty-six years old. Born in Peru, her vision is to use martial arts as a tool to empower women, specifically young minorities, to become inspiring role models in their communities.
www.kickboxers.com

Henshin

Chris Wingate

Henshin (変身) is the Japanese word for metamorphosis, meaning "to change, transform or equip the body."

My story begins in Huntington, a small suburb of Shelton, Connecticut—a sleepy little town developed from subdivided New England farmland. I was born in 1955, the middle child and the only boy.

I had no older brothers to teach me how to be tough. Growing up with four sisters, I became a gentle boy. Fighting never occurred to me when I was very young, but as soon as I reached school age, I was introduced to that experience quickly. I didn't learn how to defend myself, but I did learn how to take a great beating. I was really good at getting beat up!

When I became a preteen, I discovered television heroes who were very skilled in the fighting arts. I admired Robert Conrad's character, James West, in the TV series *The Wild Wild West*. Boy, could he fight! Later I was amazed at a small Asian actor in the film *Marlow* starring James Garner. The young Asian actor tore apart Marlow's office and jumping front kicked his chandelier, smashing it to pieces. That same Asian acted in another series, *Longstreet*—his character taught martial arts to a blind detective (Bruce Lee). A few years later Lee would star in his own martial arts movies.

In the summer of 1972, one of my friends had an introductory lesson at a new martial arts school in nearby Ansonia, Connecticut, about twenty minutes from Huntington. One afternoon he showed me and another friend some basic self-defense moves—mainly wrist breaks, wrist locks, and shoulder locks, all submission moves. My friend and I were amazed, and the very next week we went to class with him.

The new school was called Oriental Sports Training Center. The instructor was a Mr. Lee, a Taekwondo master from South Korea. That night I bought my first uniform and had my first lesson. In one hour I was hooked, and my life would change forever.

The school was in an old, second-story unit with hardwood floors. There were no windows, heat, or air-conditioning, but we didn't care. This was the place I would learn how to protect myself, which was my main goal.

I had no long-term plans, I just wanted to learn enough so that I had a little more confidence when it came getting beat up. I signed up to attend the beginner's class three times a week.

The classes were very strenuous, but that was just what I needed. I spent as much time as I could there, training with the other students. That's where I met David Wheaton, my main training partner, mentor, and lifelong friend. He became the brother I never had.

For two years we trained in Ansonia despite the horrid conditions: freezing cold temperatures in the winter and sweltering heat in the summer. It didn't matter; we learned perseverance.

When we were Blue Belts, our master started his flagship school in Branford, Connecticut, about forty-five minutes from my home. We were required to train there twice a week as well as three times a week in Ansonia. We didn't mind—we would have trained seven days a week, and we often did on our days off! We trained through all three degrees of red belt together. It was early 1974.

One day both Dave and I got the call we'd been waiting for: We were scheduled to test for black belt. Hundreds of students attended the Ansonia school, but only five made it to black belt. We were a band of brothers.

Through martial arts training, I was transformed from a weak person, physically and mentally, to a much stronger version of myself. My confidence was greatly elevated at the perfect time as I grew into manhood. This carried over into every aspect of my life.

Twenty years after my first black belt test, I graduated from the best culinary school in the country in the top 3 percent of my class. The two experiences were similar in many ways.

Becoming a Black Belt is challenging. Everyone knows it is challenging physically, but it is also challenging mentally, emotionally, and spiritually. Students discover who they really are, and the stronger they become, the more they excel.

Being a chef is not a glamorous position the way it's portrayed on celebrity cooking shows. It's an extremely challenging career, both physically and mentally. It is a really tough job. As a chef, I am constantly getting burned or cut, and I average eight to twelve miles a day walking. One has to be a culinary warrior to survive, and a strong one to excel.

My forty-two years as a Black Belt have been instrumental in my success as a culinary warrior. I can't even imagine where I would be if I hadn't pursued the path I stumbled on. It has been an amazing journey, a true metamorphosis.

Christopher Wingate has been a Black Belt for forty-two years with multiple degrees in Taekwondo and Hapkido. He graduated from the Culinary Institute of America and is a professional chef, working in management for the last twenty-five years. He resides in sunny South Florida with his wife, Yuri Harada-Wingate.

Winning Starts with Beginning

Richard Marlin

The WKF World Karate Championships, Sun City, South Africa, 1996. Every two years, the best competitors from around the world do battle for the title of World Champion. Each country sends a single competitor per weight class, only their best.

I stepped up to face the favored Italian champion, my younger, quicker, and more experienced opponent.

At forty-one years of age, I was under no illusions. A succession of coaches had told me I would never make it this far. But my long-held dream had finally arrived. I was grateful to be representing my country and was determined to give it my best shot, whatever the odds.

Ten years earlier, I had been a spectator at the 1986 World Karate Championships, and as I watched, I dared to imagine myself out on the mat, representing my country at the highest level.

It took a decade, but I was finally here. Competing in Karate for me isn't about fighting. It's about facing the unknown, testing the limits, and simply finding out what is possible. And here I was in South Africa, about to find out on the world stage.

In those days, to win the fight it was the first to reach six points. Any technique could be awarded a point (a wazari) or two (an ippon) based on difficulty, skill, and timing.

The Italian clearly believed his speed and youth would give him a natural advantage. He came at me fast. I anticipated his movement and hit him with a right reverse punch to the stomach. The referee awarded a wazari, the first point.

The Italian attacked again, even faster this time, but I caught him on the way in with another right reverse punch and gained another point.

I pulled back, luring him in, appearing hesitant, as though I was as surprised as him that I had two points already. It worked. I pushed forward and landed yet another blow. I was halfway toward winning the match!

Frustration was written all over his face.

He exploded at me again, and once more ran straight onto the same punch! Unbelievable! This was good. Now the score was 4–0. I was only two points from victory.

Just as I dared to believe I could really win, good fortune deserted me. The Italian changed tactics, got smarter. He became more careful as well as more determined. He grew in confidence, landing decisive blows.

As the tide turned, self-doubt raised its ugly head. The momentum of the match shifted as my advantage evaporated. I desperately tried to protect my score. Time seemed to slow way down.

He was all over me, pushing his newfound advantage and inexorably eating into my lead. Quickly the score became 4–1, then 4–2, then 4–3. I thought, *If I let him get to 4–4, I'm gone. It's all over.*

And sure enough, there it was: 4–4.

My heart sank. What had seemed like a possible victory only moments ago was now certain defeat. My conscious mind told me the game was up; the dream was over.

I was mentally and physically exhausted by the demands of the fight, and I resigned myself to losing.

Just then, however, when all was lost, instinct took control. I switched feet. For years I had been working on my weak side, getting that left punch to work under pressure, thousands upon thousands of repetitions.

The Italian, on the back of four unanswered points, thinking he had it all figured out, came for me. I dropped low, drove forward, and punched, left-handed for the first time in the match. I caught him cold, drilled him mid-stride. The referee awarded me an ippon—the maximum two points for a perfect technique, and a 6–4 win against one of the world's best!

I remember the very moment, at the age of nineteen, that I was introduced to the martial arts by my friend Dom Hawke. The whole thing immediately captured my imagination. I saw dignity, strength, meaningful movement, mental focus, and artistry. I walked into a Karate school, got started, and never stopped.

This was my new beginning. Little did I know the life direction that one decision would eventually take me. With that beginning, I started winning in life.

I have discovered that the number one "secret weapon" for success is: "Winning starts with beginning."

My journey in the martial arts has taught me that, regardless of age or fitness level, the only thing that can stand between me and my dreams is the procrastination that comes from fear, self-doubt, and limiting beliefs.

One of my favorite quotes is from German philosopher Johann Wolfgang von Goethe: "Whatever you can do, or dream you can, begin it. Boldness has genius, power, and magic in it."

Martial arts has given me a higher sense of purpose, harnessed my energy, kept me physically active and constantly learning. The lessons of the martial arts have proven to be an anchor in hard times, given me inspiration, and provided me with the mental focus and perseverance to overcome obstacles, strive for my dreams, and, most importantly as a teacher, help others achieve *their* potential.

The journey to the world championships was long. There were many obstacles and many doubts. And there were fears. But I never would have got to where I did, and I wouldn't have found out what was possible if I hadn't taken that first step.

Richard Marlin, the founder/master of Success Martial Arts in Lismore, Australia, has received numerous awards, including the 2010 Australian Martial Arts Professionals Award. In recent years he made an inspiring comeback, winning many martial arts events, including the 2015 National All Styles lightweight title at the unheard of age of sixty.
    www.KaratelsMore.com

A Lesson on Failure

Alex Rodriguez

I woke up one morning and realized I had failed. I had failed at creating the business I had always wanted. I felt inadequate because I was unable to take care of my family.

The year was 2008, and what happened to me and my business was part of the huge economic downturn that negatively affected many small businesses across the country. Many people lost their jobs and their homes, and in some strange way I found solace that at least that had not happened to me yet.

The only advantage I had was that I had been taught to deal with failure. I had trained in the martial arts.

I started my training when I was eight years old. I grew up in a very rough neighborhood in Southern California, and my mother, in her infinite wisdom, enrolled my brother and I in Kung Fu classes.

I received my first black belt at twelve years of age, and like a lot of other martial artists, I trained off and on for years. Some of the arts that I trained in included Tai Chi, Praying Mantis Kung Fu (and Korean Mantis Kung Fu), Wing Chun, Kenpo, and Jeet Kune Do. But when I found Hapkido, I felt like I was home.

In martial arts I learned that it was okay to get it right the first, second, or twentieth time. I learned that the important thing was to push myself and expect the best—and then it would come. I learned the skill of perseverance.

Little by little, I used that same skill to slowly dig myself out of the hole. As I looked at my business, I saw where I could make changes, and I also saw where I could not make changes and figured out ways around them. Slowly, with the patience of a white belt under the tutelage of a grandmaster, I made the necessary corrections and adapted to the new reality I was facing as a business owner. Surprisingly it all made sense on one hand, yet on the other it made no sense whatsoever—but I continued to persist.

My perseverance paid off.

I hate to fail, but I learned that it is a part of success—the yin-yang of success-failure.

My sixteen-year-old son, Joey, and I are currently third-degree black belts in Dynamic Circle Hapkido. Both Joey and I have learned and fine-tuned many skills in the dojo that we can use in the real world. In particular, the one skill that both Joey and I have continued to grow and make strides in is leadership.

For me, being a Black Belt is a humbling experience. When I received my first degree black belt I knew that I wanted to volunteer and teach others. Many people gave of their time for me to learn, and I figured that it was time for me to give back. I have been teaching ever since. I teach because it makes me a better martial artist. When I see something that needs to be corrected in another student I realize that there is an opportunity for me to improve to the next level as well.

There is no greater feeling than waking up the day after a black belt class and feeling sore muscles throughout my body. I have been fortunate to be part of a school that reinforces the health benefits of training in the martial arts and offers advice on proper nutrition in the process.

Over the past few years, I have also realized that the martial arts, at least for me, is more than physical training. When I walk onto the mat at the dojo, whether I am training or teaching, it's like walking into a temple or a church. I am able to commune with something greater than myself.

As a martial artist I have learned what compassion really means, and I try to practice it every day. I know that many times I fail, but just as I may fail at a certain technique on the mat, I continue to challenge myself so I will be better than the day before.

A few years ago I asked a man to discontinue his verbal abuse of an elderly woman at a grocery store. Once outside, the man came up and shoved me in the chest once, and then a second time. When he tried it a third time, I grabbed his hand and took him to the ground. From this pinned position I easily could have dislocated or broken his arm, but instead I asked, "Are you okay?" I was genuinely concerned for him. For me this was a lesson in compassion.

I can say that, at fifty-one years young, I am in the best shape I have ever been, both physically and spiritually, and I can attribute it to my training and the support I receive from my martial arts tribe.

I am also proud to say that I have never been in a fight. I have used my training to de-escalate a couple of situations, as well as defend myself—all without striking anyone.

I have learned over the years—although it is not always easy to accept—that it is okay to fail. Basketball great Michael Jordan once said: "It is okay to fail; everyone fails at something. What I am afraid of is not trying." This is the attitude I like to take with me everywhere, whether in business, personal relationships, or training. And it is something that I like to teach and model for students.

All of us fail. The question is: What will you do with a failure?

My answer is to learn from it and not fail in the same manner again.

A native of Southern California, Alex Rodriguez is president of Diversity Consulting Group, an advocacy and strategic communications consultancy. Alex has assisted numerous Fortune 500 companies, government agencies, and small businesses throughout his career. A lifelong martial artist, Alex is a third-degree black belt in Dynamic Circle Hapkido.
www.DCGCompanies.com

From Poverty to Possibility

Sergio Von Schmeling

My father was a proud man and chose to do things his own way. He was like a gypsy, moving his family from one place to another, until one day he decided he wanted to be a farmer. In the middle of nowhere, he built a house in the Paraguay countryside, and that's where I was born.

Our house had a bare floor with two walls of stone and the other wall, bamboo. It was nothing much for a family of ten, but we were super happy. We ate mangos, avocados, watermelons, bananas, corn, yucca root—whatever grew, we ate. And we played in the trees, day after day.

I didn't know we were poor until my father decided to move us to the city. He didn't have a job at first, and it was very hard. I was seven years old and saw other kids with houses that had floors, electricity, and running water—luxuries we did not enjoy.

I asked my mother, "How come we don't have those things?" And she answered, "We are poor."

"I don't want to be poor," I said. "How can I stop being poor? What can I do?"

My mother answered, "Well, you need to study, work hard, respect your parents, and believe in God." So that's what I did.

My father eventually found work repairing shoes, and my job was to deliver the shoes to the customer and collect payment.

The trick was how to get home with the money. I had to hide it because the other street kids constantly tried to take it away from me. I had to learn how to fight, how to kick, how to punch, and how to run . . . *fast.*

I grew up fighting on the streets, not because I was a fighter but because that was life. There were many kids working on the streets—delivering milk, selling candies or bread, shining shoes, delivering newspapers or coal for burning. Fighting was a part of everyday life.

A Catholic lady in our neighborhood had a TV, and if we agreed to pray and go to Mass with her, she would let us watch David Carradine in *Kung Fu* every Thursday. By age eleven I knew I wanted to be a master of martial arts, just like in the show.

I found a martial arts school downtown and tried to enroll, but they didn't teach children. I was persistent, though, and they finally agreed. The training was not great—having bruises everywhere was normal—but I loved it, and I never quit.

By the time I was a teenager, I felt really good about myself. I was winning tournaments and being featured on TV and in the newspaper. All of this was great, but I was still looking for my ticket out of poverty. I decided I was going to be a lawyer.

I started working for an insurance company when I was sixteen years old, and my boss was also taking martial arts classes. When I graduated high school and told him I was going to go to law school, my boss said, "You should open a martial arts school."

I replied, "No, nobody makes money in martial arts," but he told me, "You will because you're different. I will lend you the money to open your school."

So at eighteen years of age, I opened my first school. My former instructor did not want me to teach adults because he was afraid he would lose his students to me. The association would only allow me to teach women and children, and in 1983, in Paraguay, there weren't many women and children practicing martial arts.

I opened my school and used the opportunity in my classes to also teach life skills. I began to build a reputation, and within five years, I had five schools.

About that time, I was invited to compete at an ATA national tournament in the United States. On that first visit, I knew I wanted to stay.

I met Master Clark in Jacksonville, Florida, and he helped me navigate the immense immigration requirements. Master Clark was influential in my coming to America, and he is still one of the most influential people in my life.

I worked for Master Clark, and I told him I wanted to open my own school in Orlando. On March 8, 1993, I opened that school and began teaching classes, recruiting members, and training instructors. We opened another and then another, and today, we have 34 schools.

My martial arts training gave me the social skills, discipline, self-control, confidence, and self-esteem to develop a business system. I helped my instructors become successful because I understood their desire to grow—the same desires I had as a child in Paraguay.

I would say my purpose is spiritual; the goal is material. The goal is more like a reason—you have goals to fulfill your material world. Your purpose is to fulfill your spiritual world. And when they both match—when they both go hand-in-hand—you have success and happiness.

I believe the universe put me here to share. That is my purpose—to teach everybody how they can also have a successful, happy life. And it's much easier to enjoy happiness when you have some financial security and can provide for your family. You have more choices then.

America is like a buffet. You can eat everything you want. Of course you should not eat everything; you should eat what is healthy for you. But it is the biggest buffet in the world. No country in the world is like America!

Chief Master Sergio Von Schmeling is an eighth degree Black Belt and five-time world champion. He is the president and founder of Victory School of Life, with thousands of martial arts students in Florida, Texas, Michigan, Wisconsin, Arizona, Nevada, Denver and California. www.VictoryMA.com

Headstrong to Heart Strong

Amanda Arcuri

I was fifteen and had just gotten my learner's permit to drive. I asked my dad if I could borrow the car one night to go to a "sleepover" with friends ("sleepover" is teen code for "joyride, drink, and party with older kids"). My dad said no, and even though deep down I knew it was a bad idea, I was very stubborn and threw a big fit. No one was going to tell me what to do, and I decided to go anyway.

At midnight, once everyone was asleep, I stole my dad's keys and quietly backed his car out of the driveway. My plan started off great. I drove through the back roads with four of my friends to find the party. The windows were down, the music was blaring, and we were all drinking and talking and singing at the top of our lungs. I felt invincible. It especially felt good to be doing what I specifically was told not to do.

I only took my eyes off the road for a moment. I turned to say something to my friends in the backseat, and when I turned back around, I was literally on top of a sharp turn. I swerved hard, overcorrected, and skidded across the other lane . . . head-on into a tree.

My friends and I were bruised and the car was a wreck, but thankfully there were no serious injuries. I was extremely shaken up—my attitude could have gotten me and my friends killed.

Consequently, I was not allowed to drive for a few years, and all my friends got their licenses ahead of me. Lessons like this didn't need to come with such a high price, but my stubbornness always got in my way.

Growing up, it was a bit of a free-for-all; parental discipline was somewhat lacking. My single dad remarried when I was six and was also in the process of starting his own business. He traveled a lot, leaving my sister and I in our new stepmom's care.

For six years, this neurotic, overbearing, and verbally abusive woman disciplined us by trying to crush our spirits. Her attacks were endless. Constantly on edge, I developed a quick and sharp defensive nature. Being blamed for everything under the sun, being talked down to, and taking a huge hit to my self-esteem as a young girl really set me up for disaster in my teen years.

After their divorce, my dad remained single and due to his demanding work schedule, my sister and I came home after school to an empty house until he got home. Being an opportunist, I quickly realized that I could do whatever I wanted— a dangerous realization for a stubborn, trouble-making thirteen-year-old.

I made all kinds of poor choices: boys, drugs, and the wrong crowd. Oh, and don't forget the car accident. Teenage angst ensued. I had low self-esteem, a *huge* chip on my shoulder, and a general "F-you" attitude toward the world. The years spent with my critical ex-stepmom had created a monster.

Considering how defensive and stubborn I was as a teenager, I became a pretty well rounded, down-to-earth, and happy young adult. But I still had an almost debilitating stubbornness that began to cause problems in my professional life. My attitude created roadblocks as I tried to progress and create a successful future.

I found a steady job in a busy restaurant, making enough money to pay my bills and live on my own. Life was good! But something was still not right. I was still trying to cruise through life, never taking responsibility for my actions and shirking as much responsibility as possible. My attitude was, "If it's not fun and doesn't *directly* benefit me, I'm not going to do it." I was selfish.

During my fourteen years at that restaurant, I became a mother, and somehow stumbled upon the martial arts. I decided to earn my black belt. The years of training began, and the changes that began to unfold in me were staggering. I first realized something special was happening when my boss at the restaurant (who was like a second mom to me) said, "You know, Amanda, ever since you started martial arts, you just say, 'Yes, ma'am' instead of arguing about every little thing. It used to be that if I asked you to fold the napkins a new way, you argued, and had to know why, then argued more. Now you just say, 'Yes, ma'am.'"

Martial arts, in a nutshell, is what changed my life. I finally started asking myself those hard questions: *Why* do I act like this? *Why* do I think like this? *Why* am I so defensive? *Why?*

I was finally ready to stop and look inside—I was on a self-discovery journey of understanding myself, learning what I wanted, and finding peace. All of this came to me from my martial arts training.

People around me took notice because it was impossible to ignore. I began to automatically respond to others with respect and a positive attitude. Most importantly, I began to understand what it meant to be a good mom.

Considering the mother role model that I had growing up, I could have unintentionally repeated my childhood experiences with my daughter and perpetuated a cycle of abuse. However, the self-awareness and inner journey that came along with my training helped me spot old behavior patterns and stop them in their tracks.

I learned that I'm not just a headstrong tornado whirling through life, repeating my childhood experiences. Martial arts slowed the tornado, opened my heart, and gave me insight to be the person and mother I am proud to be today.

Amanda Arcuri inspires fitness and positivity as a certified instructor for Kickboxers Ultimate Training (KUT) at Martial Arts Family Fitness in Santa Barbara, California. She is a second-degree Black Belt in Dynamic Circle Hapkido, a health nut, and an awesome mom working toward her bachelor's degree.

www.getKUT.com

What a Black Belt Means to Me

Alejandro J. Zayas-Ramos, twelve years old

My black belt means that I am closer to what I want to become as I continue to grow spiritually, physically, and mentally. My black belt means three very important things to me: courage, leadership, and determination.

My black belt means courage because I have to be brave in order to test. I have to stay calm whenever I present something, both in martial arts and in school. My black belt means that I can face anything and succeed. This black belt helps me to be confident in school and in life. I feel that my black belt is a mental boost and gives me the ability to stand and fight for what I believe in.

My black belt represents leadership because I am learning to set an example for younger students. I feel that the black belt is to be respected, but so are the lower belts. Being a Black Belt means I must set an example to those who follow me.

My black belt shows my determination because I put my mind to it and have made it this far. My black belt shows me that if I believe, I can do so many things. It shows that I can set a goal, work hard for it, and succeed. My black belt is an important symbol of my determination.

I will achieve my goals. I will not give up. I will become the best I can be.

I began Taekwondo in Florida when I was five years old, and I practiced until I was seven, when my family and I moved to

Ohio. I continued training in Taekwondo, but because I was at a new school, I was demoted. I felt very sad. We left at the end of the year and went back to Miami. I continued with Taekwondo, but yet again I was demoted.

I worried that my family would move again and I would be demoted another time, but I decided that I wasn't going to let that happen. I worked harder to test more frequently, and I finally made it to black belt. I continued to train as a Black Belt until I fulfilled all the requirements for my second dan. Then my family and I moved to California. I was happy to continue training, completely forgetting to worry that I might get demoted. I began training for my second black belt, this one in Hapkido.

My Hapkido black belt means that I have written a second story—one for myself and one for everyone else. This black belt is of spiritual value to me because it contains all my hard work and all my memories in one amazing, inspiring, and incredible belt.

Achieving a black belt is physically rewarding, especially after all the hard work that goes into testing. My black belt is of sentimental value and mental value to me; it is not merely a belt. It is a story, the story of everything I've been through—every hardship, every success.

When people asks me about the black belt, they usually think it is the final belt, and there is nothing after that. But in reality, a black belt is a new beginning, a new story. There is the second, third, fourth, fifth, and sixth dan to achieve, and even more importantly, there is no such thing as too much practice.

The training itself is of value as well. It shows that, as you ascend through the belts, you stay determined. You keep practicing even if you feel like giving up. This ability to stay in the fight, even though it seems you've already lost, is the fifth tenet of martial arts, indomitable spirit.

All the tenets are important: Courtesy, to be respectful and polite. Integrity, to never lie or deceive anyone. Perseverance, to avoid stubbornness during sign-offs. Self-control, to stay focused during class when a Sensei is talking. Indomitable spirit, to persevere during the days before the test, the test itself, and life.

The tenets represent the true personality of a black belt. The tenets determine if one is ready for the test. They also represent an adaptable person. They represent someone who doesn't hold on to the past, but jumps toward the future. Adaptable people make new friends instead of moping about the ones not there. Adaptability also brings another ability: resilience. Resilience is being able to come back after a tough situation. I consider these two my sixth and seventh tenets. They represent every time in my training I was demoted and had to start over and still got my black belt.

I feel as though my black belt is not a trophy; it's not a symbol of power and authority. I think of it as a sign of passion for the martial arts. The belt is a symbol of who I really am. It is the beginning of a new life, one in which there is no fear, no inhibition. It is a visible symbol of everything I've worked so hard to achieve.

Finally, I must say that this belt is no mere belt; it is courtesy, integrity, perseverance, self-control, indomitable spirit, adaptation, and resilience, all in one. It symbolizes me, as well as every single moment that I have trained for it. A black belt can mean many things, but that's what it means to me.

Alejandro J. Zayas-Ramos tested for his black belt in Taekwondo at the age of nine, achieved his second degree at age eleven, and went on to earn his black belt in Hapkido the following year. He enjoys reading, playing video games, and practicing his martial arts forms. He wants to be a biochemist and currently attends seventh grade in Miami, Florida.

Practicing Happiness

Cynthia Rothrock

I was intrigued with the unusual-looking uniform and colored orange belt, so I decided I wanted to try Tang Soo Do. But after the first two classes, I wanted to quit.

As a preteen I had tried many sports and activities: dance, guitar, organ, baton, swimming—you name it, I tried it. The problem was that I never stuck with any of them. When I told my mom I wanted to try martial arts, she agreed as long as I promised to stick with it for the entire four-month minimum commitment.

I wasn't happy. I wanted to quit because it was hard. There was only one other female in the class, and at first I thought she was a man. She was a Black Belt and did not take me under her wing. In fact, during the second class, she kicked me in the head. I knew nothing about sparring, let alone blocking.

I begged my mom to let me quit, but she stuck to her guns since she had to pay for it.

Two months in, I still dreaded the classes. At one point I tried to break a half board (not knowing a half board is almost impossible to break) and instead broke my toe. I could not master the moves, and I felt very uncomfortable in the male-dominated class.

When I was training for my first test to get a stripe on my white belt, the teacher gave an encouraging talk about testing.

He said, "If you're a quitter and you give up, you are a loser. If you are not good, it's because you don't practice." I felt that his words was directed mainly at me, because I never practiced.

Out of embarrassment I started practicing, and it was like a miracle when I got the first kata down. As my kicks improved, I started feeling good about myself, and began working hard for my stripe. I tested and jumped straight to an orange belt. I learned an important lesson that day: You can't give up just because something is tough. You have to give it a chance.

My second lesson was learning to believe in myself. I entered a competition as an orange belt, one stripe, and I had to compete with women of all ranks. I had to compete with Black Belts—including the Black Belt from my school who had kicked me in the head. I was afraid, but instead of feeling defeated, I went out there and gave it my all.

A Black Belt took first place, and I took second place, beating out that Black Belt from my school (she took third). I was on cloud nine. This was the first time I had ever won anything. I beat people who had been training for years! It was then that I knew I could be the best in the world if I would just "practice" hard.

To be the best I had to practice and learn as much as I could, devoting every minute to martial arts. I studied in Taiwan and Hong Kong, and I even spent eight weeks in Chendu, a remote part of China where they rarely saw foreigners. Earning my black belt taught me how to set goals—and how to reach them.

Eventually I started competing on a professional basis. When I became World Champion, I set a goal to be undefeated for five consecutive years. This did not mean that I would be competing once or twice a year—we're talking thirty times a year.

It was hard to reach my goal. In my fifth and final year of competition, I received a movie offer to go to Hong Kong and work on the movie *Yes Madam* for several months. Since taking this job would conflict with reaching my goal, I asked the director to let me fly back and forth from filming so I could stay in the competition. I was lucky he said yes, but it wasn't easy. I would be on the set in Hong Kong, fly to the US on Friday, compete on Saturday, win, and then fly out Sunday and be on the set again Monday morning.

I learned to never give up on my goals and to always believe in my dreams. My dream wasn't going to just happen like magic— I had to work hard, study, train, and devote the time necessary so I could improve and stay on top. When I won, it just forced me to train harder.

Being a Black Belt gave me confidence, not only in protecting myself but in anything else I wanted to achieve. Being a Black Belt taught me to not accept failure, but to learn from it and move on. I do my best, learn from my mistakes, keep in good shape, and stay positive and happy.

Martial arts has made me the person I am today.

I am still training and doing martial arts, and I will forever. I love being able to teach others my techniques and philosophy so they can improve their lives the way I did. Martial arts is truly a gift everyone can take advantage of. Not only do we get healthy, but we become confident, strong, and a role model for others. One of the best things a producer said to me was, "I want to do a film with you because I want you to be a role model for my daughter."

I can honestly thank my mom for making me stay in martial arts. Who knows what I would be doing if I didn't stay in that Karate class? Now with five black belts, various awards from multiple Halls of Fame, I am still learning, teaching, acting in movies, and striving to be the best I can be.

My greatest pleasure in life is passing on my knowledge and sharing the idea that it doesn't matter who you are, how old you are, or what gender you are—you can do anything you want.

Be happy. Find things that make you happy, and do them. Don't dwell on negativity, and when you find something that makes you smile, laugh, or just feel good—do that. That's what I do, and I owe it to the discipline of martial arts and being a Black Belt.

Cynthia Rothrock, the "Queen of Martial Arts Films," is one of the greatest martial arts/action stars in the world. Grandmaster Rothrock holds black belts in five different disciplines, has been honored in several Hall of Fames, and is the undefeated World Karate Champion. She inspires martial artists everywhere to be their best.

www.CynthiaRothrock.org

How Martial Arts Transformed Me from a Nobody into a Somebody

Rob Colasanti

As a child growing up, life was challenging.

I was separated from my mother and siblings at the age of seven when my dad moved us from New York to Florida.

We survived on very little money. I wore generic clothes, we used coupons for anything possible, and I was in the free lunch program at school. My dad—a former construction worker who became disabled—often cut my hair in our backyard to save money. I wore a pair of thick "Coke-bottle" eyeglasses and was significantly overweight. The other kids used to call me "Fat Boy."

On top of it all, I spoke with a New York accent. All the Florida kids thought I "talked funny," and they constantly teased me about it.

Then, at age ten, I was out racing my little brown bike when I suddenly wiped out and broke my left femur.

As a result I spent the next eight months in a body cast—lying flat on my back in front of the TV, stuffing my face, and watching professional wrestling.

And when that hard, plaster-like "prison" was finally removed, I was physically weak and even more overweight than before. My gait was way off. My muscles were all out of balance. My right leg rotated outward, and I walked with a bit of a limp.

As a preteen I couldn't run, play sports, or even do the basic exercises in PE class that all the other kids could do. I was constantly bullied, made fun of, and treated like a total outcast. I was one of the most picked-on kids in school, and I even got beat up a few times.

My self-esteem was extremely low. Deep down inside I felt like a misfit . . . an outsider . . . a loser.

I seriously contemplated ending it all—and almost did one day.

MARTIAL ARTS—MY WAY OF FIGHTING BACK

By age fourteen, I was a good fifty or sixty pounds overweight, but fortunately I became extremely interested in martial arts.

I found a Karate school close to my house that was just about to open its doors for business. I talked my family into lending me money for the tuition, and I became the school's first student. To repay my family, I borrowed my grandfather's little red Craftsman lawnmower and went knocking on doors.

I literally became the neighborhood lawn boy—cutting grass for eight dollars a job—so I could pay back the loan. I didn't like doing this work, but it enabled me to fulfill my dream of learning real martial arts from a real martial arts teacher.

Since I had no social life, I trained at the Karate school six days a week.

My dad would drop me off in the early afternoon and pick me up in the evening when the school closed. I would watch classes and train for many hours per day. In fact, I was there so much that when I earned my green belt, my instructor gave me a key to the school.

Needless to say, the excess flabbiness I had been waddling around with for so long melted off my body at warp speed. My self-esteem shot through the roof. Over time, I became fast, strong, coordinated, and confident.

As a Blue Belt, I became the school's first program director. I was paid to teach introductory lessons to all new prospective students and enroll them into the school. This initiated my transformation into a leader.

Then, in 1988, at the age of eighteen, I achieved something that once seemed impossible. I earned my black belt! I immediately began teaching classes as a chief instructor and was known as "Mr. C." I was a regular guest on our school's television show, which was reaching about a quarter million people a week in the Tampa Bay area, and I became one of the most "popular kids" at my high school.

I was snapping Louisville Slugger baseball bats in half with my shin in front of crowds of amazed onlookers, breaking stacks of boards with my hands and feet, and flying through the air with superhero-like kicks.

I was once a picked-on, under-confident misfit who literally transformed into the proverbial "lean, mean fighting machine" with a twenty-nine-inch waist—a real Black Belt who walked the talk, looked the part, and hit with the power of someone twice my size. I was in shape, unstoppable, highly confident, and a role model to students of all ages. Being a bullied, ridiculed oddball was truly a thing of my past.

And then my career as a martial arts instructor was elevated to an unimaginable height . . .

FROM LAWN BOY TO MR. PRESIDENT

In 1994 my martial arts instructor created The National Association of Professional Martial Artists (NAPMA), and I became the first official employee at its launch. The company took off like a rocket, and soon I was promoted to vice president, where I served for five years. I eventually became the company's president, a position I held from 2000 to 2009.

With my direct involvement and contribution, NAPMA became the world's largest professional martial arts association, grossing millions of dollars a year.

Sometimes I shake my head when I reflect back on this fascinating journey.

At one point, the odds were very high that I'd become a failure in life. But then I started training in the martial arts. I became a tough-as-nails Black Belt with rock-solid self-esteem; a person who radiated confidence; a leader.

Before the mental and physical skills I developed through my martial arts training, I was on my way to becoming a "zero" rather than a "hero" in life.

Without that training I would never have become president of what became the premier martial arts business association in the country. I would never have become the author of several books about the martial arts, a magazine columnist, or a speaker. I would never have worked with celebrities from Jackie Chan and Jean-Claude Van Damme to Tony Robbins and Zig Ziglar.

Martial arts transformed me from a "nobody" into a "somebody" and taught me how to be successful in life . . . how to overcome any challenge . . . how to win!

Rob Colasanti is widely considered the "Ambassador of the Martial Arts." He is the former president of NAPMA and Martial Arts Professional *magazine and author of* The Martial Arts Business Bible. *A Joe Lewis Black Belt, he is a founding member of the digital marketing company Martial Arts Insider.*
www.RobColasanti.com

A Stone Boat

John Bussard

The simple truth of the matter is that martial arts saved my life. The Karate studio was my sanctuary. It gave me a place where I felt comfortable and was able to develop the confidence to do anything I wanted to do in life.

I grew up with an alcoholic mother. Her "on the wagon, off the wagon, in and out of treatment" saga wreaked havoc on me as a child. By the time I reached the age of ten, my parents were divorced. This happened back in the early 70s when people didn't get divorced, at least not anyone I knew. At the time I never received any guidance or counseling about alcoholism or the divorce that impacted my life in such a destructive way. I was embarrassed and ashamed of myself and my situation.

It was so hard on me that throughout middle school and high school only my closest friends knew about my home life. We didn't have a lot of money either, and due to the nature of what I was going through, I became a very shy and withdrawn teenager. It was difficult for me to make new friends, and I had a tough time fitting in at school. I'm sad to say that I didn't feel like I belonged anywhere.

However, all that changed when I was about sixteen years old. Around that time my brother and I used to tune in every Saturday afternoon to reruns of *Kung Fu*, the television show starring David Carradine. I felt a strong connection to his character, Caine, and it was then that I decided to start training in the martial arts.

I never wanted to hurt anyone, like Caine—all I wanted was the ability to move safely and confidently through any situation. The martial arts school I joined was headed by a very kind, wise, and wonderful master by the name of Ki Whang Kim. He was a masterful martial artist who was getting on in age and had produced many outstanding black belts before I ever walked through his doors.

At Kim Studio, no one started out with confidence, skill, or any ability for that matter. Everyone started as a novice or white belt. One of the beautiful things I learned early on about the study of martial arts is that nothing from the outside world matters.

When students arrived at the school for class, we went into the changing room, removed our shoes, clothes, and jewelry and put on the same white uniform as everyone else. The only differentiator was our belt color, and that had to be earned in class through hard work and sweat.

I realized very quickly that it didn't matter what people did for a living, what type of car they drove, how much money they had, or how many material possessions they owned. The only thing that mattered was their effort in the classroom. Through patience and training we developed our character and, just as importantly, earned and learned respect for ourselves and others.

The studio became my refuge, my hiding place from the outside world. It became my therapy where I developed many life skills in addition to my martial arts ability.

Yes, the physical training I received at Kim Studio was terrific and allowed me to win many championships. However, the confidence I developed allowed me to face some of the demons from my childhood and move through life in a much more positive way. The self-discipline I developed through training every day taught me the habits I needed to be successful. Most importantly, the determination I developed through martial arts training allowed me to acquire a "never give up" attitude that has propelled me forward in business and in life.

At one point, early in my life, I was similar to a stone boat unable to cross the sea of life. Through the help of my teachers and the lessons they instilled in me through the martial arts, I became a champion of life!

John Bussard is the founder and CEO of Kicks Karate, with thirteen locations in Maryland. He is a Harvard Business School alumnus, where he completed the prestigious Program for Leadership Development.
  www.KicksKarate.com

Finding Purpose

Ellen Reichelt

"What on earth am I doing here?"

Have you ever asked yourself that? Now in my mid-forties, I think self-reflection happens more as I head into the dreaded "middle age." As I look back, I take inventory, reflecting on how I got here and my purpose for being on this earth.

I grew up with an emotionally and physically abusive father. He often would go into a tirade and then act as if nothing happened. He would shame us into believing that it was our fault—if we were better, smarter, faster, or could work more efficiently, then he would not have to correct us so harshly. I grew believing I was damaged, unworthy, unlikable, and incapable.

Being the youngest of four kids, I was the one that watched him abuse all my siblings and my mother, and then was the sole child left to bear his paranoid rants. I also got bullied in grade school, which was an extremely lonely experience, as school was the only escape from him.

My mother was constantly afraid, and she couldn't help but instill that fear in us: fear of everyone and everything. More than anything, I feared my father.

As soon as I turned eighteen, I enrolled myself in a martial arts school. I wanted to defend myself from my father, and I did not want to end up like my mother—at the mercy of someone else.

I remember my very first class. I looked at the black belts in awe and thought to myself, *I could never be one of them.* Fear and self-doubt prevented me from considering the possibility. *I'm going to learn some techniques to protect myself, that's all,* I thought.

What I found was amazing. These people were supportive and inspirational. The Senseis, Masters, and Grandmasters each gave me a piece of themselves and their knowledge. The kicking and punching on targets helped me deal with the immense amount of anger I had buried inside as an abused child.

I could slowly feel myself transforming. I began to feel the possibility of self-confidence. How exhilarating!

The body is astounding in what it can accomplish, but without the mind believing and buying into the possibilities, the point is moot. Martial arts training helps heal the mind while honing the body. It makes for a powerfully poignant road to black belt.

To say the day of my first black belt test was like the birth of a new life for me would not even do it credit. With each subsequent degree, there are new, immense growth spurts.

I stopped the cycle of abuse. I married a wonderful man—he was the first person to really believe in me. I have a successful career, and I continue to train and teach Karate. I continue to take stock in my life by asking myself on a regular basis: What is my purpose? What is that which fulfills me? What is my passion?

It is through martial arts that I grow the most as an individual, wanting *more* for myself and *more* for others. It is an interesting paradox: "more" is not "material goods more." "More" is inner peace, balance in life, meaningful purpose, service to others, cultivating good karma, and helping people grow to their potential.

One of my black belts and I were talking the other day. This particular black belt had many of the same dark challenges that I had in my childhood. She battled a huge amount of anxiety, self-confidence issues, and fear before starting martial arts. I had worked with her at length as she trained for her first and her second degree black belt.

During my conversation with her, I suddenly realized the amount of healing that had taken place in her. She told me of the quiet in her mind she had started to experience instead of the racing mental anxiety that would typically overrun her. She shared with me how she had been instructing one of the younger junior belts in preparation for his next test and beyond.

When I heard the words she spoke, it was a déjà vu moment. I had heard these words before, almost verbatim. At the end of her story, she looked at me and smiled. She asked me if what she said sounded familiar. I nodded yes.

She told me they were the exact words I had shared with her when she was an underbelt. She cherished the words, the time, and the support I had shared with her, and they had stayed with her. She then was able to pass on what she had received to the next underbelt to help them on their journey.

She told me she would never forget my words to her, especially the part when I said, "I want you to have all that I have, and I want you to be even better than me." In that moment I became conscientiously aware of my purpose in this life. She lives that because I live that.

Powerful.

As a fifth degree Black Belt in Dynamic Circle Hapkido, Master Ellen Reichelt teaches Hapkido and self-defense seminars. A University of Connecticut graduate, she is a mechanical engineer and loves to train with her two German Shepherds.

No Leash Required

Martin Brown

I have traveled the world, lived on five continents, and entertained many amazing adventures. I love the peripatetic journey upon which I have embarked as a trial attorney in Australia and England, professional tour guide in Europe and Africa, consultant for the Sydney 2000 Olympic Games, and winemaker in California.

And yet there is one adventure that stands above the rest.

An old adage says, "You can't teach an old dog new tricks." I am certain that some fools believe this to be true, but I can tell you straight up that I do not. The older one gets, the wiser one gets; the wiser one gets, the more curious one gets; the more curious one gets, the more one learns.

When I was asked if I would like to take martial arts lessons, I said yes without hesitation. It was out of a longing to learn something new, something with deep-rooted traditions and principles and a craft that would be beneficial in my future life. And I was correct.

I received my first degree black belt in Dynamic Circle Hapkido at the sprightly age of fifty-one. A wonderful fellow student was twelve years old and received hers at the same test. In my heart I felt no older than she did, albeit the fact that my muscles felt differently. I was as delighted for her as she was for me. What an amazing moment!

My journey was not unique, not driven by necessity, and not with an overly dramatic goal in mind. I was not trying to prove anyone wrong or champion a cause . . . I was doing this for myself. What a wonderful journey it was—and what a wonderful adventure it continues to be.

In late 2013 I opened my own winery. Starting a business is an investment in time, money, and enthusiasm. It requires strategy, organization, forward planning, and execution of such plans. The task is one of some enormity, and too many times it is filled with trepidation and doubt. I knew that what I had learned—and continued to learn—as a black belt was invaluable to this end.

I am convinced that the success I have achieved would not have been possible without the practical application of the principles of my training. I was taught to leave nothing on the mat, to clear my mind of any problems before I entered the mat, and to make sure that anything less than 100 percent was not acceptable. (Now, I'm not saying I muscled my way through city planning or the Alcoholic Beverage Commission, but I was pretty damn confident when I walked through their doors to get all the approvals I needed!)

You can read any business texts, attend any motivational seminars, and listen to any experts on the topic of how to run a successful business, and I guarantee what they say is exactly what my sensei and mentors told me.

I am now my own boss, so I have to give it my all. The way I run my business is a direct reflection of the way I train as a Black Belt. I am responsible for the well-being of my staff, so I have to divorce myself from any other distracting issues. To be successful I must not leave anything out there to chance.

The art of being a leader is created and nurtured. It's not genetic. A Black Belt is a leader, on and off the mat. That cannot be more emphasized than through owning and running your own business.

The rule of perpetual motion lends itself to the thought that all things must be in motion; things can never stand still. If you are not moving forward, then, as the rule suggests, you must be moving backward. It never crossed my mind to not keep going with my martial arts training once I had attained my first-degree black belt. To some, the satisfaction of reaching this goal was enough. Good for them . . . not for me.

As I mentioned earlier, this old dog loves new tricks.

I'm confident in saying that the continuation of my training has brought me the greatest results. I am continually refining my craft, and once I humbly realized how little I knew of my craft, the more inspired I became. This transferred directly to my personal and business life.

Many people tiptoe their way through life, hoping they make it safely. This philosophy frightens me (it actually freaks me out), so the risks I take, the education I continue to embrace, and the excitement I possess is the formula I use to quash that fear.

While training in the martial arts, I cemented myself in a great community, entered into a wonderful relationship, and created peace and stability in my life. It was patently obvious that what I had found was intricately connected to my ongoing commitment to my training as a Black Belt.

I'm now working hard toward reaching my third-degree black belt. I am one cool fifty-six-year-old!

Lessons have been learned, and lessons continue to be learned by this old dog. It is a privilege to be the holder of a black belt, and it's a responsibility to share that privilege with others: students, friends, family, business associates, staff, and complete strangers.

Martin Brown has a law degree from the University of Adelaide in South Australia. He is co-owner of Kalyra Winery and owner of the newly created Area 5.1 Winery in Santa Barbara, California. Martin is a keen golfer, martial artist, dog lover, and ambassador for good cheer and fun times.

www.a51wine.com

Self-Discovery

John Cassidy

"We empower human potential and spark the adventure of self-discovery. We make the world a better place every day."

—*TopKick's Purpose Statement*

In 2013 a group of TopKick team members were selected to establish and clarify our purpose for TopKick, the company I founded in 1995. The experience empowered all of us to work toward a common goal. It really kick-started a new era for TopKick. But before I start that story, I'd like to take you back to 1988.

I was sixteen, and unbeknownst to me, Taekwondo was about to change the course of my life. On any given day you could catch me riding my bicycle throughout the neighborhood. This particular year, during my bike rides I took notice of some new construction going up. As the building neared completion, I became curious and walked into one of the businesses. I was greeted by a man who introduced himself as Master Kim. He explained that he was opening Mountain Kim Martial Arts.

Master Kim proceeded to ask me to become his first Taekwondo student. I had never seen a martial arts studio before, and this would be the first of its kind in my area. I eagerly agreed and showed up the following week ready to learn.

That year, 1988, was a unique time in my life. I was filled with a range of emotions as I watched my parents separate and divorce. Adolescence is typically a time when one tries to figure out where one fits in with the world. My family life had changed, and I perhaps was looking for a place to fit in.

Master Kim and the Taekwondo discipline taught me to take charge of the direction of my life. Regardless of my life circumstances, I learned that ultimately I had control over my own behavior. There were direct and tangible rewards in the martial arts that depended solely on the amount of effort I put in.

By no means had my own family neglected me, but Taekwondo became my extended family. Even though there was a deep language barrier between me and Master Kim, we were able to communicate through the language of Taekwondo. He taught me respect for others, humility, gentleness, leadership, peace, and so much more over the years, yet it all started with that first class.

With hard work, dedication, and daily training, I earned my black belt in two years.

THE SPARK

Our time together sparked the idea that I, too, could empower others through martial arts. Even though I only experienced a few years of training with my Master, it set me on a path of discovery that involved some of the greatest highlights of my life thus far.

At the age of twenty-four, I opened my own martial arts business, and I named the company TopKick. We went on to open seven locations in the Northern Virginia area, five of which were opened by students as franchises.

While martial arts has taught me many things in life, I value most of all the confidence and perseverance it has taught me along with giving me a purpose in my career.

Confidence from martial arts has helped me develop a personal and business mind-set that has allowed me to be willing to try new ventures and not be afraid to fail. It's not that I won't fail—it's the confidence to fail well. There is much to learn beyond one's typical comfort zones. Knowing that I could handle any obstacle was a lesson I learned early in martial arts.

This goes hand in hand with the perseverance martial arts has given me. There have been many times when it would have been easier to give up as opposed to going forward. The perseverance I've learned helps me to push through, whether it is a personal or business goal.

A NEW ERA

When we got together to establish and clarify the purpose of TopKick, it helped the business—and me personally—to know better what projects and activities were worthwhile for us to implement.

Our goal became clear: to take the lessons and missions we learn in the dojang and make an impact on our community. We believe that martial arts and its benefits translate into life lessons that can be carried throughout the world by each member.

I was inspired to create the Virtues Project at TopKick through a series at my church where the participants studied certain virtues. I felt we had an opportunity to positively influence our members, their families, and the community.

The twelve virtues we focus on at TopKick are vision, perseverance, compassion, integrity, focus, courage, gratitude, self-discipline, respect, confidence, humility, and contribution.

With the Virtue Project we intentionally wanted to have virtues as part of our curriculum. The purposed-based Virtues Project can empower people, spark their adventure of discovery about each virtue, and simultaneously make the world a better place.

Owning a business I'm passionate about is personally fulfilling, but it is my family that comes first. I am married, and we have three children. All of them play a vital part in the ways I develop my company as I continue to strive for work/life balance.

Having a personal and business vision that are so aligned makes it all work together.

I know that as I continue my journey of self-discovery, I will empower my family and my team members and students to do the same. And that means the world to me.

John Cassidy is the founder of TopKick, a martial arts franchise with seven locations in Virginia that specializes in character development through summer camp and after school programs. A fourth-degree Black Belt, John seeks opportunities to influence and inspire his team, students, fellow school owners, and his community through his purpose-driven company.

www.TopKickOnline.com

The Fear of Being Alone

Randee Layne

Let me start off by saying I never thought I'd ever try martial arts, let alone become a Black Belt.

I grew up on a farm in northern Canada, the oldest of six siblings. We were an active family, playing in the field with our animals and jumping off hay bales. After my parents divorced when I was eight, we kids stayed together on the farm with my dad, who had to work a lot. I became the leader, the problem solver, the one in charge.

In high school I was active in sports. I enjoyed playing offense and making the winning shot, but what I loved the most was being on a team; learning, growing, and encouraging each other. We were able to celebrate great wins and crushing losses—TOGETHER.

One summer vacation after tenth grade, my siblings and I decided that leaving the farm to move into the city with mom would be a great adventure. When we got home, I had the burden of giving my dad the "news." He was hysterical and threatened to call the cops. I tried to convince him that this was best for all of us, but he said, "I can't be alone! You are all I've got."

Alone. I had a fear of being alone, too. And I certainly didn't want my dad to feel alone. So . . . in that moment I decided to stay. My siblings did not.

Ironically, the next couple years I spent a lot of time alone. Driving to and from my mom's house an hour away and then back to our little shack on the farm, doing the chores, making breakfast . . . alone! I submerged myself into more team sports, even coaching all the junior leagues I could make time for, anything to relieve my sense of loneliness.

At twenty-one I decided to leave my small hometown, my hurting family, and my poor health (a result of trying to fix it all). My "team" was broken, and I didn't have any solutions. So I embarked on my journey . . . alone.

I traveled to see different friends in the States and went backpacking through Thailand before ending up in California.

It was there that I took some kickboxing classes at a martial arts studio. The only aspects of martial arts I knew before that were Bruce Lee, Chuck Norris, Karate kicks, and cool ninja moves. I had never entertained the idea of training in the martial arts until the day I found myself in a stiff, white uniform. I was so nervous, telling myself, *I'm gonna look stupid, I don't know how to do this!* and *I'm alone* . . . or so I thought.

As I learned the various techniques, I was challenged, growing, and bettering my skills. I started bonding with others through my training, and I realized that I was part of a team. But this was a different kind of team—it was a *tribe*. It wasn't just a team working together to get the ball in the hoop; it was a tribe of people striving to be the best they could be. We wanted the same things in life: Our goal wasn't merely achieving a winning score—it was winning this game of life together.

Before every class we recited our student creed, something our tribe believes in. One of the sentences was "I take care of myself so I can help take care of others." I didn't realize that in order to take care of others, I needed to do that for myself. I knew that taking care of my five younger siblings, my dad, my broken family was a priority to me, but taking care of myself wasn't on the list.

I was scared that if I took care of myself, I would have to do it alone and I wouldn't succeed. I asked myself, "Could I be that strong? Do I truly have the strength?"

During my martial arts training, we had to accomplish what often seemed like impossible challenges. Many times I was afraid when I listened to the voices in the back of my mind saying, "I can't." At my black belt test, I had to face my biggest fear of all.

I had the skills, but now I was going to be tested on inner strength. I would need to find my indomitable spirit and face my fear. I knew I would have to be my own coach, my own cheerleader—it was all up to me. So I wrote on my water bottle, TRUST YOURSELF to help remind me that "YES, I can," and "I am not alone!"

My black belt test was one of the hardest things I've ever had to do. I was physically exhausted, but I continued to tell myself, "You can do this," even though everything else inside me was saying, "No, you can't." That was the day I looked fear in the face—and conquered it.

Through martial arts, I overcame my fears, learned to trust myself and the journey, and discovered that I am not alone. I have become familiar with the emotion of fear, and when it appears directly in front of me, I'm no longer afraid.

Being a Black Belt is so much more than a bunch of badass kicks and ninja moves. It's about finding a tribe that wants to encourage you to be the best person you can possibly be . . . inside! How you take care of yourself determines how you will take care of those around you. The more you face your fears, the stronger you become.

As I continue training, I fall more in love with the fact that, while I still have fears to face, I am still on my journey and I am not afraid. I'm a Black Belt, and I continue to train my indomitable spirit. I care for myself, so I can help care for others. I trust myself and, I am not alone!

Randee Layne is a second degree Black Belt in Dynamic Circle Hapkido. She is a certified professional group fitness instructor and the director of KUT Global, an award-winning national fitness kickboxing system.

www.getKUT.com

When You're Hit on the Head, Say, "Thank You!"

Burke Franklin

Our martial arts instructor, an intense Vietnamese Vietnam War veteran, screamed at us, "Hit him in the head, wake him up!"

We had been rather mechanically throwing easy punches. But when he stepped up and decked the poor student in front, it was a wake-up call to take the blocking exercise seriously! Everybody got their noggin tagged pretty well, but we learned very quickly that we needed to be more present in order to successfully block. Since we were wearing helmets and gloves, it was more humiliating than painful, but it taught us to be quick and accurate.

I didn't dwell on the fact that I got hit in the head at practice. My attitude was "Hey, I'm glad I learned that here and not on the street." It was a painful lesson, but not nearly as painful as it could have been in real life.

That got me thinking . . .

Where else might I be just going through the motions without any intention of actual real-life application?

Likewise, how can I embrace my problems because they're there for my development and growth?

I think to myself, *Hmmm . . . what am I going to learn from this?* Anger produces nothing except something else I might regret. I now waste very little energy becoming angry. I find that the time and energy spent on anger would better be channeled toward solving the problem. Whatever it was that happened, I can do nothing else except attempt to fix it and learn something so I don't make that mistake again.

Learning doesn't have to be so painful if you're open to what the lessons can teach you. I find that my martial arts training is much more than about fighting or self-defense. There are many practical applications of a black-belt mindset in everyday situations.

As I write this, my car is in the shop. One of the sensors went bad so the engine stopped. Rather than swearing at my car for the inconvenience and cost, I choose to see it as an opportunity to consider that everything is connected. There are no accidents; this is not merely a coincidence. Perhaps this is a quiet message representing some other lesson available to me?

If I were to look at the situation with my car metaphorically, one interpretation could be that one of *my* sensors is off—that I'm insensitive to something or someone around me. The message might be that if I continue being this way, my "machine" will stop working. This "machine" could be my business, and I don't want that to stop.

This may seem like a quirky example, but let's look at where it leads.

While my car is in the shop, I decide to listen to the message that I've been driving along, building my company, and becoming insensitive to my staff. I realize that my employees have been asking me for assistance and deeper listening for a while—and I've ignored it. Nature finally came along and said, "You're not getting it, Burke. It's time for a breakdown so you'll stop."

It's actually very simple. I am literally experiencing a "sensor failure."

So, now that I hear the message, I can do something about it. I can choose to be more sensitive to my employees.

Regardless of the bill I get for my car repair, it's been an inexpensive lesson, as far as lessons from the Universe go!

The stronger the messages get, the more expensive, time-consuming, and painful they become. If I hadn't acted on that message, what would Nature do next in order for me to understand?

Naturally, we want to avoid pain, but in our haste we end up missing many significant messages. We don't learn the lessons. If we continue to dissipate our pain by blaming others or "circumstances," how can we improve ourselves? If we choose to forget about it before looking deeply into how we contributed to the situation, the lessons will become more and more expensive.

The subtle messages around us can be our guides for action. The trick is to *get* the lesson when Nature whispers . . . before we get hit on the head!

Burke Franklin is the creator and CEO of BusinessPowerTools.com, *the inventor of* BizPlanBuilder *(the popular software template for producing a comprehensive business plan), plus many other business development apps. As a second-degree Black Belt in Tae Kwon Do, Burke shares real-world lessons in his best-selling book,* Business Black Belt.
www.BusinessPowerTools.com

The Journey

Randy Reid

I was standing offstage at the 25,000-seat Coliseum in Madison, Wisconsin. I was just about to address the thousands of parents and the 167 Karate America candidates who were about to receive their black belts that evening.

A thought kept running through my mind: *How the hell did a high school dropout and street punk from southern California end up building the largest martial arts program in Wisconsin?*

Well, it's a long story, and it involves a milk carton . . .

As a child I had the unfortunate honor of being the only child of parents who didn't understand the correct way to handle a divorce. To earn the title of knucklehead, my mother thought it would be a good idea to kidnap me at age four and move across the country to California with her new husband. (The guy she ran off had an ex-wife that eventually married my dad . . . but that's another story.)

In those days, when children were kidnapped, dairy companies sometimes put their pictures on milk cartons to raise awareness, and they became known as "milk carton kids." I wasn't featured on a milk carton, but I certainly was kidnapped.

My dad found me four years later, and thus began the back-and-forth tug-of-war between my parents, which is not the best way to raise a child. Without any real parental supervision, what ensued was a pretty standard story: kid grows up confused and mad at the world. My answer was to run the streets, fight, drink, do drugs (hey, it was the 60s, man!), and basically become one of the millions of juvenile delinquents of this world.

Without any foundation of personal values, sense of purpose in life, or proper role models, I didn't have much of a chance. I wasn't exactly the well-adjusted, happy-go-lucky kid you'd want your daughter to date—but if you wanted to fight or party, I was your boy!

Then one day I walked into a martial arts school.

From the minute I stepped on the floor, I absolutely knew I'd found a home, a purpose, and a place I would never leave. I jumped in with both feet (no pun intended).

I not only trained daily, I moved into the basement of the school and became a full-fledged martial arts junkie, which was much better than the other "junkie" options available to me at the time.

I became very focused on competition. It was a way to build my confidence and self-esteem along with my strength and speed. The martial arts environment introduced me to others who were on the "right path." My old street friends drifted away, replaced by my new, goal-oriented martial arts friends.

I trained like a madman and went on to compete in martial arts tournaments, kickboxing (10–0, by golly!), and boxing. Although I was broke, those days were some of the best times of my life and make for great stories to this day.

The by-product of being a successful martial arts competitor was getting noticed by some of the "big shots" in the martial arts industry at the time, and that's how I crossed paths with John Worley. Mr. Worley had moved to the Midwest after a successful tenure with the founder of Taekwondo in the United States, Grandmaster Jhoon Rhee. Mr. Worley had developed a chain of schools in Minneapolis and, at the time, they were some of most successful in the country.

John Worley took me under his wing and tutored me in the basics of the martial arts business (for which I shall always be grateful—thank you, Mr. Worley!). My competitive career had prepared me to focus, discipline myself, and drive for success in the business world.

And it worked. I dove into the study of business: I read business magazines and business books. I visited the most successful schools in the country. I invested money in my education (and I still do), and I slowly transformed myself from a Karate competitor to a martial arts businessman.

Along the way an amazing thing happened. Just as with my journey as a martial arts athlete, I was able to meet many great mentors that taught me about business. I learned systems, marketing, management, and how to make a buck in the business world. I was now a businessman.

The year after I opened my Karate America school in the fall of 1984, a little movie called *The Karate Kid* came out. *Teenage Mutant Ninja Turtles* followed, then *Power Rangers* and whatever else Hollywood could throw into the market, and martial arts exploded!

So there I was with a black belt, a solid business education, and the same commitment to excellence and success I had developed through my martial arts training. With the help of my team, the school grew and became successful. I opened more schools and we continued to grow. My team members grew, too, eventually either buying a school from me or opening their own. Soon *their* students opened schools.

We grew the organization to over twenty-five schools at one point. We had five thousand-plus students and dominated the martial arts industry in the state of Wisconsin (and still do). As head of the organization, I had the privilege of testing all students for their black belts.

As I stood on stage that day in Madison, Wisconsin, looking out at thousands of students and parents, I thought back to the days of living in the basement of the martial arts school. I spoke from my heart about how proud I was of our students, and I spoke of my sincere hope that martial arts would enable them to be successful, just as it did for me.

I finished my speech, handed out 167 black belts, and walked out of the place a very happy guy.

Not bad for a street kid from Southern California . . .

Randy Reid is a lifelong martial artist. He is a former nationally rated tournament competitor and undefeated kickboxer with a 10–0 record. In 1984 he founded Karate America, which became the largest chain of martial arts schools in Wisconsin. Presently, he is the editor of the international online magazine Dojo Nation Times.

www.DojoNationTimes.com

On Unexpected Expectations

Mark Sylvester

One of the things I never expected to say in my adult life was, "I'm a black belt."

I didn't fully understand that forty-five minutes on the mat would become such a significant preparation for the next forty-five hours on the job. I expected what happened on the mat stayed on the mat, much like any other exercise program.

I didn't realize the tenets of the school, repeated after every session, would echo through conversations I had with clients, employees, and friends.

I am a Black Belt; I am living more and more a martial arts life. I have had ongoing discussions about what Musashi meant by the tenets: courtesy, integrity, perseverance, self-control, and indomitable spirit.

My first memory of what I thought martial arts was all about was the contained in the film, *The Karate Kid*. As a child of the sixties, becoming a part of a testosterone-driven activity was as unlikely a path as I would ever follow. I distinctly remember that first evening on the mat, in Santa Barbara, when I experienced instant peace and calm. It was completely different than I expected. I didn't miss a session for the next three years and earned my first dan at fifty-three.

Now, at sixty-three, I can see how deeply ingrained martial arts has become in my life. This feeling was completely unexpected.

I recall a conversation with my daughter, also a Black Belt, when she called to say she was "having a tough time with a client and as a result having a challenge with her boss." I listened, and when she was done, I said, "So that's what perseverance looks like?" I didn't have to repeat myself. I'm pretty sure the reference to one of our tenets wouldn't have occurred to me as she sought out more traditional fatherly comfort and advice.

I didn't expect a prospective employee would desperately want to work with us after learning that my wife and I put a higher value on these tenets than she might find at any other job. It wasn't so much that she wanted the actual job; it was more that she wanted to be at a workplace with that type of energy.

I didn't appreciate or expect the freedom and liberation I experienced once I earned my black belt. The road to the first belt had many stops along the way—things I had to learn in a particular order and manner with a corresponding mental attitude. Once I made it to the club and joined the ranks as a black belt, the rules and a preordained path evaporated. The tenets were very much in place, but the way I focused my energy and how I determined moving forward were deeply personal. It was at this point my practice became an art, and as I progressed, I found it was a way of life that has stayed with me every hour of the day.

I didn't understand how powerful an impact this practice would have on so many areas of my life. The lessons learned while I conquered the 150-plus techniques required to earn that first dan set the tone for the discipline I'd need to progress and learn other things.

I'm a lifelong learner, and the continuous exploration and practice on the mat cemented the power of repetition, what Grandmaster calls, "Seeking perfection of form."

I'm not able to *unhear* those words.

I didn't expect to experience the concept of *not-thinking*, or *reacting*, of *achieving stillness* and developing a radar to my immediate surroundings which allows me to be ready yet relaxed at any moment.

Another concept learned on the mat that transcends the dojo is called, "*Practicing the art of not getting hit.*" In literal terms this means understanding the distance to your opponent, gauging his or her energy, force, and strength, then knowing you only need to be an inch out of the way to be safe. This is so much like business. While I don't think of clients as opponents, there's a certain similarity to the psychology of prospects who are coming from a place of little trust. They will verbally jab with you. You've heard of potshots—these are meant to test your reflexes and mental agility. Once I understood this, my martial training came to my defense. I could deflect and use prospects' energy to further my own cause.

I've been in very contentious situations with multiple prospects (one could say I have not chosen my battlefield very well to situate myself with so many opponents.) It is not difficult for me, in those situations, to mentally close my eyes and visualize being surrounded by fellow students, all coming at me with weapons, testing my reflexes, my mental agility, my ability to keep calm, continue breathing, and trust my training.

I didn't expect this training on the mat to affect how I've been able to survive when dropped into a conference call with a dozen skeptical chief technology officers who were more concerned with being seen as smart and proficient among their peers than genuinely seeking the truth of the situation. Poking me to find the soft spots in my arguments was a sport for them—and unknowing to them, a sport for me as well.

I sometimes wonder if I would have been any good at martial arts when I was twenty, thirty, or forty years old. I'm extremely grateful that the stars aligned for me to meet my future wife, who led me to the mat and to Grandmaster Wheaton at a time when I still have many more years to practice and integrate the lessons learned.

As a co-founder of Wavefront, Mark Sylvester's software has revolutionized the way the world is entertained. His company introduced the world to CGI and received an Oscar. In 2015 he was awarded the California Small Business of the Year Award. As a TEDster Mark is always looking for "Ideas Worth Spreading."
www.MarkSylvester.com

The Green Belt Who Almost Lost Everything

Roland Osborne

One day the newness of martial arts training wore off for me, and it turned into work. I wanted to quit.

Whether in the middle of a race or the middle of college or the middle of anything that takes some time and work to accomplish, it's common to lose some energy. Like me, when most people hit intermediate belt in martial arts, they get bored, unfocused, tired, and burned out.

I told my dad I wanted to take a break from martial arts training, so we went to talk to my instructor, Jason Frank. He took a fun approach and said, "I know you want to play other sports and meet girls, but you will meet a lot of friends training here. You are really good—about halfway to black belt—and people who take breaks don't come back."

He made a great point, but to be honest it didn't convince me or change my feelings at all. I still felt tired and bored.

My dad then taught me one of the most important lessons of my life. He told me, "You don't want to take a break—you are just tired and a bit lazy. Honestly, we all get tired, but that doesn't mean we quit or take a long break. The truth is, people are tired when they get up to go to work, but they still go. You will get burned out and tired no matter what you do. Successful people break through these small times of burnout, and they eventually go away. You just have to keep going."

That didn't change the way I felt. I still didn't want to go. He was stern, though, and basically said, "Get your belt on and go to class." For a few weeks I tried not to try in class. I also tried on a little attitude, but that wasn't any fun.

One day it hit me. I was sitting in class and thought, *Actually, I'm really lucky to be learning how to fight, get stronger, and earn a black belt. How cool is that? No one else in my regular school is doing that. Other sports are cool, but they aren't learning how to fight and protect themselves. I'm going to be such a better person for doing this.*

Then I thought, *Why should people force me to be good, to do something cool? They shouldn't—I should be excited to be doing this.*

I became grateful, got remotivated, and realized that this was what I really wanted. I learned how to persevere, even when I didn't feel like it.

I see this happen all the time now. People have not learned this habit of perseverance and determination. They haven't recognized how much gratitude helps to get out of a burnout. When we focus on the positive things that come out of a situation, it inspires us!

I appreciate my dad teaching me about dedication and perseverance and making goals a reality (not a wish). Now I know there is nothing I can't do. Every goal I set is a goal I will get. I understand that, when I sit down to do something big, I will get burned out at some point; people and other things will try to stop me. I'm prepared to take on big challenges and burnouts to accomplish big goals and achievements.

If my dad had let me quit that day, I have no idea what I would be doing now. I know it wouldn't be traveling the world, training with top instructors, involved in amazing projects, or talking to you.

I see so many people go through this cycle of mediocrity. They start, then stop; start, then stop. Every time something gets a little difficult or they get a little tired, they stop.

But it doesn't have to be this way. You don't have to settle for mediocrity in your life. You can find your determination point and get through the small burnouts. When you do this, you will be unstoppable. Write down your goals and dreams, and be ready to break through your temporary burnouts to achieve them.

Roland Osborne is a martial arts Black Belt and has traveled the world training with many high-level athletes and instructors. He has taught over 150,000 people and certified over 10,000 trainers. He has a TV show on the Discovery Channel, has won at over 150 tournaments, runs several martial arts businesses, and motivates thousands of martial arts schools and instructors weekly. His life mission is to reach, teach, and inspire as many people as possible.

www.RolandOsborne.com

The Skeptical Black Belt, or
How I Learned to Stop Worrying
and Love the (Ugh) Journey

Raymond Janik

Fair warning: I'm not much of an inspiration. I didn't grow up wanting to be a martial artist. I'm not super athletic. I wasn't looking to change my life, become a better person, or begin a (ugh) journey. I haven't even been a black belt for very long. There are people with more impressive skills and stories. I won't feel bad if you skip to theirs; I probably would.

So, this is a story for people who don't have athletic glory days to remember; those of us for whom the best part of a workout is finishing. It's especially for those of us who shudder a little when people talk about their "journey" in social media posts with lots of pictures of rainbows and sunsets.

Closing in on fifty and bored with my workout routine, I signed up for a fitness program at a gym that also taught martial arts. Everyone there was enthusiastic and so . . . nice. The vibe wasn't like any gym I'd ever been to, and it definitely was not what I expected from a "dojo." I'd only ever experienced that level of enthusiasm from people on commission.

I thought I was in okay shape, but quickly learned that I'd been going pretty easy on myself when working out alone. Kickboxing was undeniably cool: we all harbor at least a little action movie hero-envy, right? Backfists and sidekicks on a bag are a pretty safe way to indulge that, even though I was far from stellar at it, but even as I started to understand the basic techniques, I also saw some people around me who had noticeably better form. Their kicks and punches were combined with intention and flow, and most of them were staying after classes to do actual martial arts.

I was intrigued—but also more than a little dubious. My not-at-all-extensive knowledge of martial arts came from movies and TV. There would be blind obedience and arduous physical effort and some philosophy and not much fun, right? There were creeds and tenets posted on the walls, and the students recited them—vigorously—at each class. *Not for me*, I thought.

Remember those nice people at the dojo? Wait till you tell them that maybe—just maybe—you're considering giving a martial arts class a try. They weren't pushy; they just couldn't contain their enthusiasm. I figured I'd give the month-long intro class a try.

Right off I found myself doing things I thought would feel silly. There was bowing, those creeds and tenets, calling each other "sir" and "ma'am." Weird at first, but I came to appreciate it. I found it was a way to get, and keep, my head in the game. It took real focus, the kind you can't fake. The instructors were surprisingly patient and, truly, some of the best teachers I'd ever seen. They would explain a technique in as many different ways as it took for me to learn it. And they seemed genuinely pleased when I finally got it.

It wasn't all serious business, though. I trained with youngsters and women about half my size who were skilled and fearless and could seriously kick my butt. And I got to break a board! I still have it, and it seems laughably thin now, but it was one of the coolest things I'd ever done. I saw people who had been training for a little while or a long time, and I wondered what it would be like when I got my next belt, and the next one after that.

I expected the physical training to be challenging, and it was, but I could handle that. The real challenges came from unexpected quarters. Like I said, I'd seen the movies and TV shows. But there was no posturing by the instructors, no hazing from other students; nobody tried to hurt anybody else. I kept waiting for something to happen so I could say, "Aha! I knew this was all a scam." But it never did. Everybody stayed nice and supportive and enthusiastic.

I started to feel like I was the one faking it. Like there were expectations I wasn't meeting. It's easy to tell if someone is doing a front punch properly. It's trickier to tell if someone is acting with integrity (one of the tenets). I assumed others said the words but didn't spend a lot of time trying to integrate them into their training or their lives like, well, me. I wasn't a terrible person, but I wasn't working as hard to try to improve in these intangible areas as I was in demonstrating my skills. I don't know if other people could tell that, but I could.

As I mulled that over, I was introduced to the concept of *seeking perfection of form*. The Grandmaster talked about always trying to make his basic techniques better. I began to see that it wasn't just about kicks, throws, or strikes. Our creed and our tenets were things we would never perfect but could always keep working toward. It didn't matter if anyone else was faking it (they weren't). It only mattered if I was—so I decided I wouldn't.

I started doing things I "didn't do." I unabashedly referred to myself as a martial artist. If anyone asked me about my training, I sounded like the people I'd met when I first started training: "You have to try it—it's so great!"

I began to assist with classes, and I found I looked forward to that almost as much as my own classes. When students mastered a technique, or were promoted, I was filled with pride for them and inspired by their efforts.

And (suddenly) after years of training, I was a Black Belt. I haven't had a chance to put my action-hero skills to use—yet—and I'll probably never post a picture of a cat in a gi on my Facebook feed, but *becoming* a Black Belt and *being* a Black Belt have permeated my life for years now and changed not only who I am, but who I want to be. Kicking and punching are great, but, as corny as it sounds, seeking to embody tenets like courtesy and integrity, while always challenging, enhances the experience in ways I never imagined.

I roll my eyes less at "journeys" now. Clichés become clichés because they're true. As with all good journeys, the best part isn't the destination—it really is all about what's discovered along the way.

Raymond Janik is the clinical training administrator for Fielding Graduate University in Santa Barbara, California. When he's not administrating, he trains in Hapkido, scuba dives, and travels whenever he can. His wife calls him "Li'l Ninja."

Failing for Good

Alexandria Buzzell

I have loved martial arts my whole life. It has brought me my greatest rewards, but also the greatest failure of my entire life.

As a five-year-old, I watched my neighbors walk up the street to their Karate school, wishing I could join them. Ironically, my parents wanted me to get involved in something I could turn into a career, so they weren't really interested in me learning martial arts. Instead I got into music and played piano and cello, and I sang.

One day when I was sixteen, my friend invited me to attend one of his Karate classes as a guest. I loved it and made a pitch to my parents. I told them I had saved up some babysitting money, and if they let me take Karate lessons, I would pay for them myself. I was hoping this would make it hard for them to say no.

As it turns out, it was. In fact, my mother, brother, and sister took the class with me. My mother said, "We're all going to do this together," so my siblings and I got a paper route to earn money to pay for our classes.

I was homeschooled, and one of the house rules was that I couldn't go out until my lessons for the day were completed. My Karate lesson was at 9:00 a.m., so I woke up at 4:30 or 5:00 a.m. each day to get my lessons done beforehand. I would jump on my bike for a seven-mile ride, and most days I would stay at the school all day for training. I practically lived there.

By the time I graduated high school, I was competing. I also got certified as a personal trainer so I could work out all the time in order to become a better competitor.

I started out competing in local Karate tournaments. I trained in Tang Soo Do and competed in Kata, Kama, Bo, and fighting. In 1997 I made it to Team USA and competed in Hungary.

I loved martial arts so much that I made it my career, first as a head instructor for many years, and as the owner of a martial arts school with my husband.

I had earned my third-degree black belt when I was twenty-four, so I set a goal for myself to earn my fourth-degree by the time I was thirty. I knew that this was 100 percent achievable, but while I was training for the test, my husband and I decided to open our own school. This meant that there was no one to promote me, and it would take a lot of time and focus. I thought I might have to adjust or postpone my chance for promotion, but Master Garcia came to the rescue and said he would test me when the time came.

Thus my training continued until . . . I hurt my ankle. I ended up on crutches for three months! However, I was not going to let this setback stop me. After all, I was a black belt competitor and black belts don't give up. I recovered and trained as hard as I could for six months until the day of my test finally arrived.

I was excited. The test started with pad work, followed by self-defense techniques, knife attacks, gun attacks—all which I had practiced. I was sweating and panting hard from three hours of giving it my all when Master Garcia interrupted the test to pull me aside. He said, "I just don't think you're ready."

Wow. I was devastated. All the hard work I had put in was not enough. I was also embarrassed. I had told so many people, including my students, that I was taking the test, so it felt terrible to fail so publicly.

I left the floor. I was in shock. I still couldn't believe I had actually failed.

I spent the rest of the weekend in my room in tears. I experienced a cascade of emotions—including anger when I started thinking, "It's not fair!" I felt humiliated that I had let my students down. They had been cheering me on and supporting me through the whole training process. Even as I licked my wounds, many of them were sending messages of congratulations, not knowing I had failed.

Then came the self-doubt. Would I ever have what it takes? I mean, here I was, a school owner—had I reached the end of my training line? Up until that point, I had always been at the top of my class; it had all come easily. Would I ever be ready for my fourth degree? I knew I had trained with everything I had, so how would a few more months make a difference?

One thing Master Garcia said to me was, "When you pass this test, you will not just be one of the few fourth degrees in the organization—you will be the only female." I realized that this test wasn't just about me. I was setting an example for my students, but also for all of the students in our organization.

So I gave myself a few days to grieve and process, and then I did what Black Belts do. I got back to training, specifically focusing on the areas I needed to improve.

Six months later I took the test again. This time my intensity, confidence, and technique was at a completely different level. I was so grateful for my instructor's wisdom in forcing me to push just a little bit further and not accept "good enough" as a standard.

The experience of failure made me stronger. Since then, I, too, have had to pull people aside to tell them they weren't ready to promote. My own failure helped me handle the situation more skillfully because I could empathize with their situation and the disappointment they were experiencing.

I'm unstoppable! I plan to continue on as long as I can—training and making each day better than the day before. There is always more to learn, and I love every minute of the black belt lifestyle.

Alexandria Buzzell is a Black Belt and master instructor of multiple schools in Massachusetts. She has trained in a large range of martial arts from Tang Soo Do to Krav Maga. She recently opened The Martial Arts Buzz, a company dedicated to helping other school owners. Alexandria is married with two sons.

www.abdshrewsbury.com

A Mother's Lie

John Harak

A 3:00 a.m. house fire nearly claimed our lives in Derby, Connecticut, when I was five years old. This tragic event made us nomadic for nearly a year before we finally settled in Orange, Connecticut.

My dad was forced to work a variety of jobs, and one day he died of a heart attack during an afternoon meeting in Derby. The youngest of five kids, I was the last to see him that day.

Deep sadness and depression settled in me. As my mother found comfort in food, I followed suit. My resulting obesity caused me to become the subject of ridicule and isolation among my classmates and friends.

I spent a lot of time alone. I enjoyed taking various things apart and putting them back together. I also enjoyed fishing in the local ponds and streams, but watching TV while eating was my most frequent activity.

An encounter in the Bradlees Department Store in Derby sent me into an even deeper depression. I ran into a couple of my former classmates, one of whom had been a very close friend prior to my father's death. I was excited to reconnect, but when she saw me and the weight I had gained, she looked at me in disgust, said, "Ewww," and walked away.

I struggled in school. Concentration, comprehension, and retention were difficult for me. For three years after my father's passing, my mother tried to get me to spend time with relatives and engage in various activities, such as Boy Scouts, but nothing helped to put an end to my depression.

My brother Phil convinced my mother to enroll me in Karate. She thought it was a good idea and told me to be home no later than 4:30 p.m. so we could get there in time for class at 5:00 p.m. I purposely came home at 5:30, as I wanted no part of that. She said, "Come on, let's go."

"Wait—you said it started at 5:00," I protested.

She said, "It starts at 6:00, and we are going." She confessed that she intentionally told me the earlier time when she saw my initial reaction.

The school was on Main Street in Derby, and Master Tae Lee was the instructor. At the enrollment, I had to write down my age, height, and weight. I was thirteen, five foot two, and 188 pounds. I was awkward and clumsy, and I wanted to stay in the back of the class so as not to draw too much attention to myself. I couldn't do much of the warm-up exercises and was easily winded.

To my surprise, everyone I encountered was friendly, warm, welcoming, and patient. That first class went by quickly. I was impressed by the skills of the instructors, and I wanted to go back. I had no high hopes for myself that first night, but I was attracted to the people and how accepting they were of me.

The second night, my self-defense partner was David W. Dave and I had no idea at the time, but that was the beginning of a friendship that has lasted over forty years.

As the months progressed I formed deeper friendships with my Karate classmates. Many even offered to stay after class to help me. My Karate family helped me focus on my health and well-being. Friendships deepened as my technique developed along with my mind and body strength.

My strength and confidence grew stronger and stronger. Meditation, concentration, focus, integrity, perseverance, pride, and purpose were truly transformed by Karate. My school grades rose from Cs to As. My social life outside of my Karate family also grew.

I honestly don't know what would have happened if I hadn't attended that first Karate class. I later developed teaching skills as a Karate instructor that gave me the ability to speak and engage with others at all levels.

Today, as a successful professional in the hospitality industry, I continue to use what I learned in those early training years in martial arts: care for others, attention to detail, focus and discipline, cause and effect, action and reaction, and patience and persistence.

I can't imagine what my life would be like without Karate.

John Harak has served as a leader in the hotel industry most of his life, and was one of the youngest general managers at the age of twenty-five. He is currently the operations manager, food and beverage, at Walt Disney World in Florida, where he enjoys life with his wife and two children.

The Power of Forgiveness

Stephen C. Ray

It was a beautiful, sunny afternoon. Both my kids were swimming while I caught up on some reading poolside. There were several families enjoying our apartment pool area as well as two couples over in the corner. As they drank their beer, they got louder and their language became more colorful.

I went over to them and made a friendly request to stop using that language in front of the kids. One of the guys shrugged his shoulders and said, "Alright, man," and I went back and sat down. A few minutes later the profanity started again. I went over and asked him kindly to stop, and this time he got mad. He stood up, got in my face, and said, "I can f-ing say what I want to say because I am an f-ing adult."

He continued to yell and then started pounding his finger on my chest. I pushed him away, and he flew back about fifteen feet and fell over some white stacking chairs. He picked one up and ran at me, intending to smash it over my head. I shook my finger from side to side to signify that this was not a good idea; however, he proceeded to advance. Once he got close to me with the chair raised over his head, I performed a crescent kick and broke the chair out of his hands. His girlfriend grabbed him, and they left, obviously shaken.

I calmly went back to my children and jumped in the pool. About thirty minutes later the guy came back because he forgot something. As he walked passed me, he said sheepishly, "Sorry about that, man."

I smiled and said, "I forgive you."

Forgiveness has not always come easy for me. As a young boy I would listen to my stepfather beating my mother in the other room. All I could do was lie on my bed and cry, wishing for the day that I was old enough to do something about it.

My mother divorced him and remarried when I was seven. I began to watch martial arts films and loved Ninja movies and the David Carradine *Kung Fu* episodes on TV. When I met a karate instructor across the back alley from my house, I started to train enthusiastically.

I quickly became very passionate about learning martial arts. I even put together my own little neighborhood ninja group. I would teach the other kids how to swing on ropes, use nunchakus, throw Chinese stars and wrist darts, and walk on rice paper without leaving a trace (or so I thought, LOL). I would also teach them how to jump from roof to roof and then roll when hitting the ground.

We all thought it was great fun, but one time we got into a little trouble and the police chased after us. We hurdled the fences (in our little ninja uniforms, of course) and turned to see them slowly trying to climb over them. They didn't have a chance.

As I entered my teen years, I became more rebellious and stopped listening to my parents. I started smoking and swearing and hanging out with the wrong crowd. Thankfully when I turned sixteen, I met an amazing Kung Fu master and began to train under him. I became more passionate than ever before. Interestingly, none of my instructors up until this time had ever taught me anything about values, morals, or godliness. It had all been about physical techniques; however, this teacher taught me positive life principles. Eventually I earned my teaching certificate.

My life changed even more when, at the age of twenty-one, I met a woman who brought me to a nondenominational church.

There I prayed for Jesus Christ to come into my heart and be my Lord and Savior. I became a new person in Christ Jesus.

Through prayer, my purpose in martial arts became: "to help as many people as possible reach their greatest potential by helping them grow spiritually, mentally, and physically." And that is what I have done, and continue to do. I have had the amazing opportunity over the years to use martial arts to help people who would never attend a church.

To me, my walk with God and my martial arts walk are synonymous. Martial arts provided the necessary life skills I needed to be successful. I learned to be my best by developing spiritually, mentally, and physically. Training as a Christian has helped me to internalize values such as respect, focus, confidence, humility, humbleness, perseverance, a desire for excellence—and, of course, forgiveness.

Stephen C. Ray is a sixth-degree martial arts master and founder of FIT Martial Arts in St. Louis, Missouri. He is the bishop of fifteen churches, an orphan home in India, and a church in St. Louis, where he lives with his three children and two grandchildren.
    www.fitmartialarts.com

110 Percent

Mike Hieshima

In 2011, during a routine hip replacement surgery, I experienced complications including two cardiac arrests and a major stroke on the right side of my brain. It left my left side nearly paralyzed and caused a condition called left side neglect (meaning that the brain ignores anything in the left visual field). This experience was devastating and left me with tremendous anxiety and depression.

As background, I am a fifty-year-old martial artist, the father of two Black Belts (my proudest treasures), and have been a student of Hapkido for over twenty-five years. I currently hold the rank of fifth dan black belt and train at Martial Arts Family Fitness (home of Hapkido International) in Santa Barbara, California.

Martial arts ingrained in me the values of perseverance and indomitable spirit. While in recovery, my fellow students and the grand master visited me many times. It was through this energy, caring, and help that I set a goal of being better than I was before the stroke.

The first challenge I had to face was learning to walk and function again. My condition resulted in weakness and coordination issues. I went to Hapkido class and watched other students move. I would visualize my movements before the stroke and began to see new levels of flow and energy. The more I watched, the greater my determination to return grew. I couldn't wait until my hip healed enough to allow me to try even basic movements.

Several months of watching finally came to an end as the doctors gave the okay to start training again. My issue was not only physical—it was mental as well. I needed to get in better shape.

I decided to enroll in the KUT program (Kickboxers Ultimate Training) to increase my fitness through exercise and diet. This was incredibly challenging for me, as I was humbled by the difficulty in performing simple hand strikes and kicks that I had done thousands of times before. The combinations, the music, and my physical limitations were almost too much to bear, and I found myself almost tuning out multiple times.

What saved me was the progress I was making on the fitness side. In a ninety-day period, I went from 185 pounds and 21 percent body fat to 165 pounds and 11 percent body fat. My speed, energy, and spirit progressed as I become more fit. This gave me the confidence to step back on the mat for the first time and participate in a class.

It was a day to remember, as I was humbled by the welcome I received and the care I truly felt from my martial arts family. It required me to step off the mat briefly to wipe away the tears. At first my movements were clumsy and uncoordinated. My ego began to take over, leaving me feeling like a white belt again. But by the end of class (once I stopped thinking and just found the void of emptiness), my movements started to flow.

It took several more months before all cylinders were firing, but more and more frequently I found myself moving better, faster, and in different ways than I ever had before. Practicing using weapons on my left side proved to be incredible therapy and helped immensely.

Today I continue to make progress and improve every time I'm on the mat. People say I haven't lost a step and move better than ever. Without martial arts, Hapkido, and KUT, there is no way I could have reached this level.

I get asked regularly about the degree of my recovery. My answer without hesitation is 110 percent!

Mike Hieshima is president and chairman of the nation's top retail brokerage network, ChainLinks Retail Advisors. He is a twenty-seven-year veteran of retail commercial real estate and a partner with The Shopping Center Group in California. He has multifaceted expertise both locally and nationally with a focus on strategic expansion of retailers and landlord representation.

CAN'T Is a Four-Letter Word

Bill "Superfoot" Wallace

It was a career-ending injury. The doctors gave me a 50/50 chance of ever being able to use my knee again. It happened in November 1966 when I was practicing for the California State Judo Championships.

I weighed 150 pounds and had been training with a guy thirty or forty pounds heavier. I came in for a throw called a Tai Otoshi, which is like a body drop. He stepped over my leg to counter it, so I stepped through his leg to do what it is called a Kouchi Gari, which is like a trip. He collapsed and fell on my right knee. And that was that.

My medial collateral ligament was torn, and I was put in a cast from my ankle all the way up to my hipbone. I figured that any chance for the career I wanted, or any training that I ever wanted to do, was gone.

While I was still in the cast, a friend of mine said, "Hey, there's a Karate school downtown. Let's go check it out." I said, "Okay," and off we went.

The instructor said, "You wanna do Karate?"

I answered, "Sir, I wanna do Karate."

He said, "Stand up. We're gonna do it now."

I said, "I can't. I'm in a cast."

He said, "Ah! It's okay. You stand up. I teach you Yoko-Geri."

I asked, "What the heck is a Yoko-Geri?" It turns out it was a sidekick. We did that about fifty thousand times. Then he said, "Now we're gonna do the Mawashi Geri."

I said, "Okay. What's a Mawashi Geri?" A roundhouse kick. I did that one fifty thousand times, too. I could only kick with my left leg, but pretty soon, I was really, really good with that left leg.

I was in a cast from November until February, and during that time I practiced a total of two kicks. I couldn't punch, or throw, or do anything else. What I could do was stand there and throw a sidekick and a front roundhouse kick.

After I finally got out of the cast, I started sparring a little. One day a guy came in with a kick and I threw a sidekick at him, but I missed and whopped him in the chest with my heel. He said, "What the heck was that?"

I said, "I don't know."

He replied, "That's a hook right there!"

So now I had a sidekick, a front kick, and a hook kick. And because I would never be able to use my right leg due to the ligament knee damage I sustained, I had to somehow compensate for it. So I made those three kicks look the same: The sidekick looked like the roundhouse kick, the roundhouse kick looked like the hook kick, and the hook kick looked like the sidekick. I knew that if my opponents didn't know what kick I was throwing, it would be hard for them to defend themselves. They would have to wait for me to throw it before they could block it, and by the time they decided to block, it would already be three-fourths of the way there.

My father wanted me to be a teacher. Instead I became a fighter. For three years I was the national champion in points fighting: 1971, 1972, and 1973. I won the first PKA Middle Weight Karate Championship on September 14, 1974. I defended my title twenty-two times all over the world: Monte Carlo, Paris, England, New York's Madison Square Gardens, Los Angeles, and Florida. I had a blast. It was that sidekick that began it all for me. It wasn't hard—it was just quick.

I learned that it is important to know what your weaknesses and limitations are so you can find a way around them. In a way, it's accepting them that allows you to use them for your strategy.

When I first started martial arts training, I knew I couldn't do anything with my right leg. It did a great job of holding me up, but I couldn't kick with it. Therefore, I had to overcome that limitation and find a way to use it as an advantage. I could only use one leg, so I had to learn how to modify my movements.

For instance, while my single leg kicks were fast, I was not a good puncher. This was a problem because certain people could get inside my leg. So I worked on developing my jab and left hook in order to keep my opponent away from me so I could use my kicking techniques.

I learned to box for two reasons: 1. To keep them away from me so I could kick. 2. To keep them away from me so I could kick.

We can modify and adapt the same way in life. If we know something won't work, great! That's how we learn. It's like Edison with the lightbulb: He didn't have 10,000 failures; he learned 10,000 different ways the lightbulb wouldn't work. Then he found one way that did.

A Black Belt is just a White Belt (a brand-new student) that kept plugging away, kept plugging away, kept plugging away . . . and kept getting a little bit better every day, a little bit stronger, a little bit faster, a little more flexible.

Martial arts is not merely about fighting. It's about peace of mind. When I was in high school and it came time to talk in front of my class, I was sick with nerves. I was not a speaker. I could never talk in front of people because I was scared and nervous. Through martial arts, I'm never really afraid of anything anymore. I'm not afraid to talk in front of people now. I'm not afraid to make appearances. Martial arts built up my confidence and self-esteem, and now I feel that I can handle anything.

Very few people can do what they really love and have it be their livelihood. Luckily for me, this is what I want to do, forever and ever and ever. My father wanted me to be a teacher. Well, I am a teacher—maybe not the kind he imagined, but I know he's happy right now.

Bill "Superfoot" Wallace retired as the undefeated Professional Karate Association Middleweight Champion and has received numerous Hall of Fame honors from around the world. He is an author with a master's degree in kinesiology, has created several training video series, and been in close to twenty films. He continues to be involved in the entertainment industry, make appearances, and conduct seminars across the globe.

www.Superfoot.com

Healing the Soul

Sara Urquidez

It was quiet. Too quiet.

I clutched my purse a little closer as I walked toward my car in the underground parking structure. The energy felt odd and made me uncomfortable. I looked around but saw no one.

As I reached to open my car door, a hand suddenly grabbed my shoulder from behind. The hand was heavy, so I knew it was a man, and as I turned he said, "Give me your purse." Instinctively, I palmed him to the chest and kicked him in the groin. As he fled, I jumped in my car and drove away.

It all happened so fast that I didn't have time to think. My body simply did what it had been trained to do. I responded with action instead of reacting with panic or fear.

I am so grateful for the martial arts. My training has helped me to be responsive rather than reactive; it has brought calmness to my soul and has taught me to be in my awareness.

I was fifteen years old when three of my brothers started taking martial arts classes. They decided to play matchmaker and would come home from class saying, "You have to meet our instructor! He is the best! He is so amazing!"

So I went with them to class one day, and there he was: "Mr. Casanova." He seemed very slick and was clearly popular with the women. He came up to me and said, "Hello, my name is Sensei Benny." I was very soft-spoken and said, "Hello." He took my hand and kissed it.

Oh, my! "I don't know you," I said, and left. As far as I was concerned, that was that.

One day my brothers came home and said, "You have to come with us. Sensei Benny has been in a motorcycle accident."

I was born with spiritual gifts, including the gift of healing, and felt responsible to help if I could. So my mother and I joined my brothers and went to Benny's house. He was lying in bed, surrounded by women.

Eventually we had a moment to ourselves so I could work with him, and he kissed me again—on the lips this time. *I can't believe this guy!* I thought. I pushed him away and told my mom, "Let's go; I don't want to be here."

I didn't like him and I didn't like his reputation, yet he would constantly show up at our house. He was always kind and considerate and fun. Gradually I saw something deeper in him and decided to give him a chance.

Two weeks after I graduated from high school, we were married. We went to Hawaii for our honeymoon . . . which just "so happened" to coincide with Benny's first professional full-contact Martial Arts World Championship.

"This is a martial arts family, and you have to keep up," Benny told me.

He couldn't teach me because we were too close, so his brother Reuben and his sister, Lily, became my teachers. I had such a great time, and before I knew it, I got my black belt and started to teach.

To this day, martial arts is a foundation for me. It is a great tool to keep practicing and become more aware, more fearless and more confident. Confidence detracts negativity. For instance, when a woman holds herself with confidence, she is seen as "not weak." She is actually perceived as a warrior. A predator knows that there is something about this woman—perhaps she has a gun—and does not want to engage with her. She holds herself with confidence and trusts that confidence completely.

That day in the underground parking lot, I responded with confidence. Yes, martial arts equipped me with physical skills and techniques, but it also gave me the internal strength I needed.

Through my teaching, healing, and ceremonial work, I use my gifts to facilitate a way of life that elevates others to the highest degree of light and consciousness. Honoring the Apache blood running through me, I respect the ways of the Native American traditions and invoke the teaching modalities of the indigenous ways into Universal Shamanism for modern society. I am a conduit for divine healing, messages, blessings, and guidance.

Martial arts brought out my natural gifts of intuition and healing in an even stronger way. For me, the arts are another modality of healing the soul.

Sara Eaglewoman Urquidez is known by many as the Urban Shaman, one who practices the ancient ways to heal and transform in today's world. She is described by those who have experienced her work as a "Miracle Worker," "Holy Woman," and a "Doctor of the Soul."
www.saraeaglewoman.com

The Principle of Flow

Derek Carlson

Throughout my martial arts training, I have had the privilege of sparring with many advanced Black Belts who helped me become better by always giving me their best. In other words, I didn't often come out ahead, but I sure learned a lot.

Every time I trained, I refined my attacks to the point where I occasionally would score—but only occasionally. Although my movements and attacks were precise and strong, they remained defensible.

I finally realized that what I believed was my greatest strength was actually a weakness because of its predictability. If I wanted to achieve true mastery, I would need to change my mind-set from mastering a specific attack to being in the flow of the match—ready to change my preferred attacks in order to take advantage of the opportunities before me.

Most people reasonably think that a strike coming in their direction is a very bad thing with negative consequences. In Hapkido I learned that a strike coming in my direction is an opportunity to harness that energy and use it to my advantage. In fact, by harnessing and working with the energy I encounter, I become more powerful than if I try to exert my force directly against that energy.

With this in mind, during my next sparring session, I decided to let go of my preferred attacks and flow with the match. My opponent, an excellent kicker, had always scored on me with quick kicks as I would advance in my attack. So this time I did not advance. I stayed at a distance in order to look for other opportunities.

Since I was not advancing, he became the aggressor, throwing kicks just out of range. My usual answer to this would have been to respond with my own kicking attack, but that would again play into his preferred counterstrikes. Instead, on his next attack, I shot inside his kick and took him down totally unexpectedly. It was a smooth and unforced movement because it was exactly what the situation called for.

I'm sure he was a little shocked, so I helped him up and went for round two. This time I came straight at him aggressively and landed a jab-cross-roundhouse combination. This was one of the same combinations he had easily defended when it was all he had to worry about. But now, with the takedown fresh in his mind, my preferred combination was less predictable—and, again, exactly what was called for in the flow of this second match.

I believe this principal of flow transcends all aspects of life. I am much more powerful and effective when I can flow with what comes at me and look for the advantage or opportunity in each situation that presents itself. I lose my opportunity to secure an advantage when I label something as negative and freeze in its path. I am much more powerful and open to opportunity when I accept situations for what they are without labeling them, and then work with that energy or situation to create the best outcome.

I also have learned to apply the principal of flow in my professional life.

One of my responsibilities is to negotiate contracts with governments for both services and development projects. A recent opportunity brought me to the table with four different governments, a competitor, and several consultants, all trying to negotiate a single development and operations contract.

The process began with the governmental agencies requesting a proposal, and our competitor submitted one first. In order to protect our business interests, we submitted a counterproposal. Over the next twelve months, we went head-to-head with the other company, competing for superiority. This competition did not come cheap as the project required property acquisition, engineering, environmental impact reports, development fees, permitting, and so on. It was becoming a battle with no end in sight; both of us went on the offensive as we tried to one-up each other.

With over a year invested into the proposal phase of this project, we needed to evaluate whether our strategy was the most effective approach. With situational awareness and flexibility of approach in mind, we assessed the situation with an open mind and determined that we would step back and look for other openings to achieve our goal.

Stepping into the flow, we determined that instead of continuing an adversarial relationship, we would explore the possibility of converting the competitor into a partner. Both parties brought separate strengths to the project that could be more focused by sharing appropriate responsibilities.

The result was that, instead of having a competitor in the marketplace, we had a new partner who strengthened our position. This never would have been possible had we continued to work on refining our "attack."

At the beginning of my martial arts training, I was looking to recapture the childhood joy of competition and physical activity. I was seeking the prestige of being a Black Belt. And, in part, I received those things, but I also received so much more. The joy of competition and physical fitness became much deeper as I expanded all my opportunities by embracing the flow of life.

Derek Carlson lives with his family in Santa Barbara, California, and is a third-degree Black Belt in Dynamic Circle Hapkido at Martial Arts Family Fitness.

Tapping into Your Black-Belt Vein of Gold

Barry A. Broughton, PhD

At o'dark-thirty, I'm hanging upside down with my shins grinding against the steel hatch opening of a M1 Abrams battle tank turret, the cries for "MEDIC!" still ringing in my ears. *What the hell have I gotten myself into?* It's day one of my first deployment.

"LT, these guys need medevaced out of here ASAP," I yell up to the guy holding my ankles. I improvise a cervical collar from a wire ladder splint and then begin lifting the tank commander's broken and bloodied six-foot, 190-pound body from where he'd collapsed into the gunner's station at the bottom the tank. The rim of the tank hatch digs deeper into my tibias as they drag me and my patient up and out of the tank hatch.

The physically demanding and emotionally intense thirty-minute evacuation now seems like hours as I replay the scene in my head. *How did I pull that off? I'm just a lost kid from nowhere.*

The searing pain in my lower legs reminds me of clashing shins while blocking kicks back home, stateside, at the dojo.

And then I realize . . . *that's* how I pulled this off.

Thank you, Kwai Chang Caine and Billy Jack. When I was that lost kid struggling through school and life, those guys were my heroes. They did the *right* thing even when it was the *hardest* thing to do. They focused, found calm in the midst of chaos, and took deliberate action. I admired their amazing martial prowess, and I was especially drawn to the inner peace that both heroes maintained in the midst of the violence and chaos they faced. Dealing with my own inner turmoil at the time, I wanted to acquire that same duality of peace and power. So I took the first step in taking charge of my life and found a dojo—and the piece of my life that was missing.

While sweating, breaking boards—and bones—I filled the void in my life with training and studying martial arts. As my skill grew and I attained my first black belt, my confidence grew as well. My martial arts family was supportive, and I began to understand that relationships forged through years of training together are often stronger than bonds of blood.

Several years after graduating high school, I realized the only way to "get out" of rural Western New York was to get an education. My only option was to do it on Uncle Sam's dime. Six months after joining the army, I started college courses on post. I approached the classes with a zeal that was far from my young teenage self who settled for mediocrity. As a black belt, I understood that it was my own internal motivators that needed to drive me, not the hope for external affirmations that might never come.

At night in my bunk, I would envision that I'd already attained my goal. Much like breaking a concrete block while training in the dojo, in my mind's eye I would visualize what I wanted to accomplish. Not only did I see the end result, but just as I *felt* the block crumble around my fist, I would *feel* and *live* my success. Although it seemed like a pipe dream at the time, I saw myself as an officer and a doctor.

I attacked Basic Training and Combat Medic training with the newfound confidence that allowed me to excel and graduate both with honors. As I stood on the stage with my fellow honor graduates, I wondered, *How did I pull this off?*

It was lessons learned from those old heroes of mine that pushed me forward when army duty got demanding and eight years of maintaining a nearly 4.0 GPA was kicking my backside. Billy and Caine wouldn't have backed down from that challenge. They would take any action necessary to complete the task. That mind-set enabled me to become a battalion medical officer, complete a two-year orthopedic surgery PA residency training, and ultimately obtain my PhD.

I had no idea I was stepping onto a train carrying me down the wrong track.

I willingly took the ride for many years, and though I enjoyed helping people, each stop took me further from my passion. After twenty-five-years in healthcare and medicine, my practice was draining me. Jumping off the career-path train is extremely difficult, and the longer you ride, the greater your speed. For me, the potential for injury from the jump was less terrifying than suffering a slow death from starving my spirit. By day, I felt like a tightly bound corpse in a white lab coat as I treated patients in my office or made rounds at the hospital. By night, I came to life at the dojo, teaching and practicing martial arts.

To give up the prestige and financial security of a career in medicine to teach martial arts full time seemed crazy to my family and friends. It was a huge risk. And without action, it would simply remain an empty wish. My thoughts and life were in constant conflict and chaos. Should I stay on the train and die a slow death—or leap and risk everything? What would Billy and Caine do?

They would jump from the damn train.

Standing in the OR, operating on an Olympic athlete who'd sustained multiple fractures during a race and was now back for more surgery, I found myself awed—and envious—of his dedication and willingness to sacrifice all for his passion. I found my answer.

I took off my lab coat and jumped from the train. I allowed my state and national licenses and certifications to expire. I burned bridges so there was no safety net . . . no turning back. I did the right thing when it was the hardest thing to do. Like Billy and Caine, I took action.

A warrior is not defined by his skill set, but by his mind-set—a mindset of action. Like Billy and Caine, there will be times in your life when you'll need to tap into that vein of black-belt gold, the one that runs through every warrior willing to "engage in the face of eminent danger." You must make the hard choices. You must take action.

Best-selling author of Beyond Self-Defense, *Grandmaster Barry A. Broughton, PhD, is the founder of AKT Combatives. Featured in The Martial Directory, he has been inducted into multiple Martial Arts Halls of Fame and is currently the Northeast Region Director for the US Sport Jujitsu Association.*

www.AKTcombatives.com

Enough!

Melodee Meyer

I opened my eyes; it was pitch black. I could barely breathe—
something was covering my face and pressing down on my head.
I tried to get it off me, but my arms were stuck. I was buried alive.

Or was I? *Perhaps he really did it this time. Perhaps this
is what it feels like when you're dead. Did he finally follow
through with his threats?*

Then I heard him. Over the sounds of shattering glass, his
voice bellowed—half yelling, half singing, like a Southern
preacher on a Sunday morning. *Okay, so I'm still alive, but
where am I? What happened?*

Oh, dear. I am under the bed. Had I crawled under it to
hide? No. He must have flipped it over on me when I passed
out. I really screwed up this time. I had fallen asleep while he
was still in the middle of one of his "episodes." I mistakenly
thought this one was winding down, and after two days of no
sleep, my body betrayed me.

The weight of the mattress, box spring, and bed frame was
crushing my legs, and I began to panic. *The baby! Where is the
baby?*

When I was younger, no one had ever heard of the term
"bipolar." Mental illness was not something that happened to
regular people, and certainly couldn't apply to the charismatic,
God-loving man I had married. Or so I thought.

The physical abuse did not start suddenly. It was a slow progression that began with words and posturing—what I recognize now as typical bully behavior. Young and naïve, I thought I was doing something wrong to make this happen.

As it got worse, I tried to stand up for myself by pushing back, which only escalated the terror and gave me more reasons to blame myself. He told me that I was not a good enough wife or a good enough mother, again and again until I believed him.

When I finally wriggled and pushed my way out from under the bed, I knew I needed to get help for me and my son, who was still sleeping soundly in the next room. Wearing nothing but my high school jersey, I ran out of the house barefoot, in the middle of the winter night, to get assistance from a kind neighbor.

That, of course, is not the end of the story—not by a long shot. It took years for me to drum up the courage to leave that relationship. I had more visits to the emergency room to endure, a stay at a women's shelter, and the experience of having all my possessions burned on the lawn to go through yet. I had more growing and learning to do.

When I was ready, I also needed some healing. Surprisingly, I got some of that on the floor of a martial arts school.

Most people know that martial arts help build confidence and self-esteem. However, for me, it had the exact opposite effect initially. When I began martial arts as an adult in my mid-thirties, I had no idea what I was doing, and with each move I felt a little bit more inadequate and self-conscious.

I compared myself to others and often felt discouraged that I was not "good enough." My sons seemed to pick it up immediately, but I felt like a fish out of water.

I remember thinking, "This isn't for me. Besides, I don't believe in fighting."

I don't know why I continued. Maybe because I didn't want to be a quitter. Maybe because I liked that we were doing something as a family. Maybe because I liked how the training was making my body stronger. All I know is that one day it all made sense.

I was talking with a wise martial arts master and told him my reservations about martial arts and the idea of fighting. He smiled kindly and said, "You must learn to fight so that you can stop the fight." *What? Stop what fight?* I wasn't fighting anymore. I had left the abuse and fighting in the past . . . or had I?

Yes, I had left the physical fight of an abusive relationship, but there remained a battle within. There was still a voice telling me that I was not good enough, that I was not fast enough, not pretty enough, not smart enough. I was continuing the cycle of abuse with negative self-talk and zero self-value.

Interestingly enough, somewhere deep inside I actually believed that this kind of self-belittling would somehow motivate me to be better, but of course it never did. I had to find a new way. I had to learn to fight—so I could stop the fight.

I trained and trained. I made mistakes so many times that I got used to the feeling of failure; instead of feeling bad about it, I would just shrug my shoulders and say, "Go again," until I got it. Training for my black belt was a long, challenging journey, but I knew I had to keep showing up. So I did.

The lessons I learned on the mat were lessons I could take off the mat into the rest of my life. I could make mistakes, shrug them off, and go again.

I wish I could say that when the day for my black belt test arrived, I was confident. But I was not. I was dealing with two injuries, and I was extremely nervous to test in front of a distinguished black belt examination board of world champions, celebrities, masters, and grandmasters. Yikes.

Was it the best test ever? Um, no. Did I do my very best? Yes, I did. Most importantly, there were no excuses to be made because . . . I was good enough. Not just to the test board and attending students, but to *me*.

Being "good enough" might seem like a subpar achievement to those who strive for being "the best." But for a young woman who did not know her worth, it was an exceptional feeling to suddenly believe in her heart the honorable mantra: *"I am enough."*

To me, being the best is not about doing better than everyone else. It is about being the best inside myself. And no outward achievement can give that to me. If I want to get better at anything, it's simple: I must practice. (Learning to love the practice is the secret.)

Even now, each time I get on the mat, I have the opportunity to reconnect with that part of me that was enough, that is enough, and that will always be enough. It can still be a challenge—but that's why the training never ends.

Melodee Meyer is a feisty speaker, fifth-degree Black Belt and BodyLove Coach who has taught thousands of folks how to love themselves lean, fit and healthy. Through her radio show, seminars, and mentoring services, she empowers hungry leaders and passionate entrepreneurs to create the life they want, in a body they love, so they can go out and change the world.

www.MasterMel.com

CPSIA information can be obtained
at www.ICGtesting.com
Printed in the USA
FSOW04n1013061216
28199FS